Cambridge Elements

Elements in Epistemology
edited by
Stephen Hetherington
University of New South Wales, Sydney

AESTHETIC KNOWLEDGE

Jon Robson
University of Nottingham

Shaftesbury Road, Cambridge CB2 8EA, United Kingdom

One Liberty Plaza, 20th Floor, New York, NY 10006, USA

477 Williamstown Road, Port Melbourne, VIC 3207, Australia

314–321, 3rd Floor, Plot 3, Splendor Forum, Jasola District Centre, New Delhi – 110025, India

103 Penang Road, #05–06/07, Visioncrest Commercial, Singapore 238467

Cambridge University Press is part of Cambridge University Press & Assessment, a department of the University of Cambridge.

We share the University's mission to contribute to society through the pursuit of education, learning and research at the highest international levels of excellence.

www.cambridge.org
Information on this title: www.cambridge.org/9781009571777

DOI: 10.1017/9781009358521

© Jon Robson 2025

This publication is in copyright. Subject to statutory exception and to the provisions of relevant collective licensing agreements, no reproduction of any part may take place without the written permission of Cambridge University Press & Assessment.

When citing this work, please include a reference to the DOI 10.1017/9781009358521

First published 2025

A catalogue record for this publication is available from the British Library

ISBN 978-1-009-57177-7 Hardback
ISBN 978-1-009-35851-4 Paperback
ISSN 2398-0567 (online)
ISSN 2514-3832 (print)

Cambridge University Press & Assessment has no responsibility for the persistence or accuracy of URLs for external or third-party internet websites referred to in this publication and does not guarantee that any content on such websites is, or will remain, accurate or appropriate.

For EU product safety concerns, contact us at Calle de José Abascal, 56, 1°, 28003 Madrid, Spain, or email eugpsr@cambridge.org

Aesthetic Knowledge

Elements in Epistemology

DOI: 10.1017/9781009358521
First published online: October 2025

Jon Robson
University of Nottingham
Author for correspondence: Jon Robson, Jonathan.Robson@nottingham.ac.uk

Abstract: How do we arrive at aesthetic knowledge? This might seem an odd question for philosophers to ask. Some will take its answer to be obvious: we learn about the aesthetic qualities of paintings by looking at them, of musical works by listening to them, and so on. Others will take the question to be misguided, how can there be aesthetic knowledge when aesthetics is merely 'a matter of taste'? Finally, aesthetic knowledge itself might seem singularly unimportant. We don't engage with beautiful artworks to learn that they're beautiful but, rather, to appreciate that beauty. This Element argues that each of these objections is misplaced. Aesthetic knowledge is both valuable and attainable, but canonical philosophical (and folk) views of how we attain it are mistaken. The Element surveys some recent arguments against the reliability of aesthetic perception and in favour of other, more social, sources of aesthetic knowledge.

Keywords: Aesthetics, epistemology, art, testimony, acquaintance

© Jon Robson 2025

ISBNs: 9781009571777 (HB), 9781009358514 (PB), 9781009358521 (OC)
ISSNs: 2398-0567 (online), 2514-3832 (print)

Contents

1 Some Orthodoxies of Aesthetic Knowledge   1

2 The Problems of Aesthetic Perception   9

3 Disputing about Taste   23

4 Aesthetic Knowledge: How to Get It
 and Why You Want It   38

   References   55

1 Some Orthodoxies of Aesthetic Knowledge

This Element is about aesthetic knowledge, how we get in, and why we might value it. Does it make sense to enquire into such matters though? We can reasonably ask how the art historian arrives at knowledge of the background of various artistic movements or what methods cognitive scientists can best employ to arrive at knowledge of what certain groups tend to find aesthetically pleasing, but investigating aesthetic knowledge itself is liable to appear rather more suspect. This Element will be structured around considering three pieces of folk wisdom which might be taken to preclude the very possibility of a substantive enquiry into aesthetic knowledge.

First, we might be concerned that identifying the process of acquiring aesthetic knowledge is just 'too easy' to warrant any serious investigation: we learn about the aesthetic qualities of paintings by looking at them, of musical works by listening to them and so on. Second, it could be objected that – given that aesthetic judgements are merely 'a matter of taste' – talk about knowledge is misguided. When I say 'the painting is beautiful' I am merely expressing my opinion, just as you are when you say that 'the painting is ugly'. There is no shared 'fact of the matter' here about which either of us could reasonably make a claim to knowledge. Finally, we might think that aesthetic knowledge, if such exists, is too trivial a thing to be worthy of serious study. This is not to say that the critic here thinks the aesthetic itself is unimportant, far from it, but merely that the value of our engagement with art works isn't found in the acquisition of knowledge (or at least not knowledge of this kind). We don't spend time reading novels, gazing at sunsets or listening to music because we want to learn *facts* about the aesthetic value of these objects.

Given the topic of this work, it is unsurprising that I don't find any of the aforementioned considerations convincing as reasons to foreswear serious investigation into aesthetic knowledge. Why though? Do I think that the claims themselves are unconvincing or merely that they fail to provide appropriate support for the further contention that we should regard questions concerning aesthetic knowledge as trivial, unimportant, or impossible to answer? The answer to this will depend on which claim we are talking about as well as the details of how we interpret it. Each of these claims has been taken to be an obvious piece of common sense, and it also seems that each also has prominent philosophical defenders. As we will see, though, things aren't always that simple. It is true, for example, that some prominent philosophers of art (Goldman 1995, Young 1997) have defended relativist accounts of aesthetic judgement, but these are often considerably removed from the kind of relativism which many lay people are inclined to accept (or, at least, which philosophers are inclined to take them to be inclined to accept). Aestheticians who endorse views such as aesthetic relativism typically won't take this to reduce such judgements to mere matters of opinion over which there can never be sensible disputes (what they *do* say will be the focus of much of Section 3).

In this Element I hope to shed light on the nature and value of aesthetic knowledge by arguing that each of these apparent truisms is either mistaken or best interpreted in a way which doesn't conflict with the legitimacy of serious enquiry into aesthetic knowledge. I begin, in Section 2, by arguing that the question of how we come to have aesthetic knowledge isn't as easy to answer at it has seemed to many to be. The obvious 'easy answer' here is that we paradigmatically learn about aesthetic matters via perception. Whether there are other means of acquiring aesthetic knowledge is, as we will see, controversial, but the fact that perception is the best route, epistemically and otherwise, to such knowledge is often taken to be too obvious to stand in need of serious defence. I will, however, argue that this claim to epistemic superiority, far from being obvious, is actually mistaken. Perception isn't an especially reliable route to aesthetic knowledge (especially when it comes to complex art works) and social factors, such as testimony, are able to provide us with a far more secure epistemic position. Section 3 argues that accounts of the semantics of aesthetic judgements which take them to mere matters of opinion, or otherwise incapable of attaining the status of (substantive) knowledge, are uniformly implausible. This is not to say that views such as subjectivism are implausible but, rather, that the kinds of subjectivism which philosophically minded subjectivists adopt have surprisingly little impact on our general understanding of the nature and extent of aesthetic knowledge. In Section 4 I say something more positive about how I think aesthetic knowledge is best acquired (again, stressing the role of social factors here) before going on to explain why I take such knowledge to be of more value than has typically been supposed. I will say a little more about each of these claims, and the plan for subsequent sections, later. First, though, it's worth getting a little clearer as to the overall topic of this work.

1.1 Aesthetic Epistemology

The primary focus of this work is how we can come to know the truth of various aesthetic judgements. If I tell you that Varo's *Naturaleza muerta resucitando* is an excellent painting, that the Trevi Fountain is beautiful, and that the taste of Old Roan cheese is exquisite, how can you come to *know* whether any of these claims are true? Before answering this question, we need to think more about what an aesthetic judgement even is.

An obvious answer to this question is that aesthetic judgements are judgements about the presence (or absence) of aesthetic properties in an object. While I believe this answer is – at least when suitably finessed – correct, it is hardly an informative one without understanding more about aesthetic properties themselves. Luckily, examples of aesthetic properties are easy to come by, and it is largely uncontroversial that properties such as beauty, ugliness, gracefulness, elegance, and sublimity all qualify (at least, that is, if we take 'property' here in fairly minimalist sense which doesn't entail any metaphysical commitment to aesthetic realism). While examples are easy to come by, offering a satisfactory definition is a much harder matter and any attempt to do so at this stage would likely beg some important questions. Given this, I will forebear from attempting to formulate one (though for some accounts of the nature of aesthetic properties see Levinson 2005, Matravers 2005 and De Clercq 2008) and content myself with highlighting some key points of controversy.

A first question to consider is what we take the scope of the aesthetic to be. I have suggested that certain claims about how an object tastes are genuinely aesthetic, but this has been disputed and some (e.g., Scruton 1979: 114) are inclined to restrict the aesthetic to the so-called 'higher senses' such as vision and audition. Similarly, I have included *being an excellent painting* as an aesthetic property, but some would likely be inclined to think of this as an artistic, rather than aesthetic, property (Hanson 2013). On one account of the distinction, an artistic property would, roughly, be any property which we could use to evaluate an artwork as an artwork (rather than as, say, an investment or a way to cover up damage to a wall), whereas aesthetic properties are required to be straightforwardly perceptual in a way which properties such as being excellent, original, or humorous are not (for some concerns about this distinction see Lopes 2011). I won't attempt to settle the substantive debates on these issues here though. I will tend to focus on a relatively wide range of putative aesthetic properties in this work but very little hangs on this. Those inclined to be rather more selective about what they count as aesthetic can easily substitute their own examples.

There is also a related debate about which kinds of object can instantiate aesthetic properties. Since at least the early modern period, the history of aesthetics has tended to focus primarily on artworks (though discussion of the aesthetics of nature also played a significant role). However, recent work in aesthetics has opened up a far wider range of objects for discussion. In particular, the focus on 'everyday aesthetics' has considered the putatively aesthetic qualities of practices ranging over clothing choice (Shin 2022), puzzle solving (Kubala 2023), eating and drinking (Korsmeyer 2002), sports (Borge 2019), and the use of recreational drugs (Nguyen forthcoming). This project of widening the scope of the aesthetic has, however, proved rather controversial (for more on the scope and nature of the project see Saito 2015 and Dowling 2010). For the purposes of this work, I will aim to dodge controversy by largely focusing on the aesthetic properties of artworks. However, I don't mean to suggest that these other items aren't capable of instantiating genuinely aesthetic properties.

Having said a little about the 'aesthetic' part of 'aesthetic judgement', it's also worth being clear about the 'judgement' part. As with 'aesthetic', this term gets used in a variety of different ways by philosophers (see, e.g., Shah and Velleman 2005: 503). In terms of the current debate, though, the question of what an aesthetic judgement is has generally been taken to be the question of what the mental correlate of an aesthetic assertion is. As Gorodeisky and Marcus (2018: 139) put things

> the debate about the nature of aesthetic judgment concerns what state of mind is expressed by statements such as "North by Northwest is excellent" as they occur in paradigmatic contexts—for example, in critical discussions of the value of artworks. The technical term 'aesthetic judgment' refers to whatever is thereby expressed.

As parallel discussions in metaethics make clear, a little more would need to be said here. For example, we will need to focus not just on the mental states of someone who makes aesthetic statements in general (even if we restrict ourselves to paradigm contexts as they suggest) but on 'someone who competently, sincerely and without delusion about their own state of mind utters' these statements (Ridge 2009: 198).

This common ground helps us to get clear on the nature of the debate over aesthetic judgement, but it still leaves room for significant debate as to the mental states which play this role. Are they beliefs (in a straightforwardly cognitive sense), some conative state such as a desire, a certain kind of pleasure, or something else entirely? For most of this work I will talk as if aesthetic judgements are straightforward beliefs differing only in content (rather than fundamental nature) from ordinary beliefs about shapes and colours, cars and trains, planets, and protons. This might seem to beg some important questions in the current debate, but I will argue in Section 3 that this framing makes surprisingly little difference and that all of the conclusions I reach are equally available to, for example, various kinds of expressivism in aesthetics.

Having discussed the nature of aesthetic judgement, a further question is why I've chosen to focus on *knowledge* of such judgements. It would not have been too long ago that this question, in a work of epistemology, would seem out of place. Isn't knowledge just what epistemology is about? However, much recent work in epistemology has argued that there are various important epistemic questions which don't take (propositional) knowledge as their focus. Questions concerning, understanding (Grimm 2012), knowledge how (Brogaard 2012) – assuming that we reject views (such as those of Stanley and Williamson 2001) which take knowledge how to be a kind of propositional knowledge – and epistemic values more broadly (Pritchard 2007). I don't mean to deny that any of these are worthy of study and will suggest in Section 4 that the focus of aesthetic epistemology has, in several respects, been unduly narrow. However, I will also suggest there that consideration of these other questions does nothing to undermine the value of aesthetic knowledge (or the study of the same).

A final issue is why we should take there to be anything interesting to say about *aesthetic* knowledge in particular. After all, much work in epistemology seems to assume that epistemic questions are relatively topic neutral, and we wouldn't expect separate works on the nature of knowledge, the value of testimony or the significance of peer disagreement for every individual domain of knowledge. A popular answer to this question would be that aesthetic epistemology *is* different. Most obviously, there are a range of famous claims which suggest, at least if we interpret them epistemically, that the legitimate routes to knowledge in aesthetics are far narrower than they are elsewhere. For example, Tormey (1973: 39) claims that 'In art, unlike the law, we do not admit judgments in the absence of direct or immediate experience' and Wollheim's (1980: 233) that 'judgements of aesthetic value ... must be based on first-hand experience of their objects'. I will return to claims of this kind later in this work but, since I take them to be substantially mistaken, I cannot rely on this explanation for the interest of aesthetic epistemology as a topic. Instead, I believe that the primary reason for such an interest is that so many – in both philosophy departments and Clapham omnibuses – have *taken* aesthetic knowledge to be different. Understanding why they have been mistaken will (in my humble opinion at least) in my (perhaps starting to look rather less humble) view allow me to highlight some important truths about the nature of aesthetics and suggest fruitful avenues which philosophers should pursue in future.

1.2 Claim One: Perception Is Obviously the Most Reliable Route to Aesthetic Knowledge

How do we come to know that, say, a specific painting possesses a particular aesthetic property such as beauty? The answer seems obvious: you look at the painting itself. Aesthetics, we have been told – going back at least as far as Baumgarten (1758) co-opting the term as a name for his new 'science of perception' – is about a particular kind of sensory perception (see, e.g., Nanay

2016 and Margolis 1960). Beyond that point of agreement, though, things get rather more controversial.

We might agree that we should judge a painting by looking at it but precisely what this amounts to has been the subject of a great deal of debate. Indeed, the question of how 'picture perception' works has become a mainstay of recent philosophical aesthetics (see, e.g., Korsmeyer 1979, Lopes 1996 and Ferretti 2017). These debates are certainly interesting ones, but in this Element at least, I won't be pursuing them – nor parallel debates concerning, for example, whether we can literally hear sadness in music (Davies 1980, Radford 1989). Rather, my focus will merely be on the general idea that it is easy to identify perception, however it operates, as the most reliable source of aesthetic knowledge concerning certain artworks.

I say 'certain artworks' here since there are famous concerns about how widely views of this kind can be applied, with philosophers of art pointing to examples – such as certain works of literature (Shelley 2003: 373–375), and of conceptual art (Hanson 2015) – where it is either difficult to see what perceiving the work would amount to or else where perception doesn't seem to play a particularly crucial role in evaluating it. I will, however, ignore such claims in what follows and focus on cases where the claim seems to be at its strongest. That is, works which look to be straightforwardly perceptual and where perceiving them (or at least a very close surrogate such as reproduction or accurate photograph) seems to be a pre-requisite for evaluating the works for ourselves. Even here, though, I will argue that the claim regarding perception is mistaken. It isn't obviously true that perception is the most reliable route to aesthetic knowledge because it isn't *even* true that perception is the most reliable route to aesthetic knowledge.

The next section will focus on Claim One and argue that, at least in many cases involving complex artworks, perception is surprisingly unreliable as a route to aesthetic knowledge. As such, I will argue that it is not obviously, and indeed not actually, the most reliable route to aesthetic knowledge. My argument for this will incorporate both traditional philosophical arguments (dating back at least as far as Hume) as well as the results of more recent empirical work. The section doesn't argue for a complete scepticism regarding aesthetic knowledge from perception, but it does suggest that our epistemic position here is rather weaker than many of us ordinarily believe. I then go on to suggest another means of acquiring aesthetic knowledge, based on something like appeal to the test of time, which I take to be far more reliable.

1.3 Claim Two: Aesthetic Judgement Is Merely 'A Matter of Opinion', Making Aesthetic Knowledge Either Impossible or Trivial

The idea that aesthetic judgements are just 'a matter of opinion' is a rather common one. Indeed, it might seem that this is just what being an issue of taste (including aesthetic taste) means. As the title of this section makes clear, though, there are two importantly different ways in which this claim could be interpreted. The first of these maintains that, since aesthetic judgement is a 'mere matter of taste', it makes no sense to talk about knowledge here. The second interpretation allows that aesthetic knowledge is possible but argues that it is a trivial matter to obtain it. For me to have aesthetic knowledge is just for me to know that I personally like something or take pleasure in it or find it beautiful or ..., where this is something which I have privileged access to simply by introspecting my own mental states.

Before we can assess either interpretation of the claim, though, we need to ask what it means to talk about aesthetic judgement being a matter of opinion. We might, perhaps, want to spell this out in terms of the judgements in question being in some way relative, subjective or merely the expression of feeling. As we will see in Section 3, though, there are a range of different ways of explicating each of these views. Further, even when the nature of these views is agreed upon, their proponents face the difficulty of balancing our apparently conflicting intuitions when it comes to aesthetic matters. Young (1997: 9) frames things this way in his discussion of relativism.

> On the one hand, it often seems that *de gustibus non est disputandum*. If so, pretty much any aesthetic judgment is as good as any other. On the other hand, as Hume also recognized, we have a competing, equally compelling intuition: some artworks are better than others, and some aesthetic judgments are mistaken, no matter what anyone thinks. By any reasonable standard, Milton really is a better poet than Ogilvy, Bach is a better composer than Fux, and Austen's novels are superior to Barbara Cartland's.

It isn't my purpose in this work to either endorse or reject any particular response to these puzzling issues. Rather, Section 3 focuses on targeting Claim Two and argues that, once we focus on the most plausible contemporary versions of these views, they make surprisingly little difference to the main positions I am defending. That is, each of the competing positions will allow that we can have substantive knowledge (in a sense I will explain further in Section 3) of the aesthetic and that this knowledge frequently isn't a trivial matter to acquire. Finally, I will suggest that each of these views is compatible with appeal to social factors of various kinds as important routes to aesthetic knowledge.

1.4 Claim Three: There Is Little Value in the Mere Acquisition of Aesthetic Knowledge

The final claim that I will be rejecting is the idea that there is little value to merely acquiring aesthetic knowledge. Again, though it's important to be clear about the scope of this claim. The suggestion is not that knowledge *tout court* is irrelevant when it comes to our engagement with art works. Appreciation of *Hamilton,* for example, is likely to be enhanced by, amongst other things, knowledge of the histories of the American Revolution and the conventions of both hip-hop and musical theatre. More controversially, a number of philosophers have suggested that a significant part of the value of engaging with certain kinds of artworks lies in the knowledge (or other cognitive values) they can provide us with. In particular, it has been argued (Green 2017, Carr 2021) that narrative artworks can provide us with valuable insights into important topics such as character. Rather, the claim is merely that there is very little value to our acquiring specifically aesthetic knowledge from engaging with artworks. That is, that there is little value merely in knowing which aesthetic properties particular works possess.

Why might someone think this? The obvious answer is that the key element(s) of our aesthetic engagement is something besides knowledge, the most prominent candidate being a certain kind of appreciation (though some, e.g., Gorodeisky and Marcus (2018) take knowledge and appreciation to be rather more closely linked than I am suggesting). When philosophers talk about appreciation, they typically mean something like perceiving the aesthetic qualities of a work 'as realized in the work' (Budd 2003: 392) or 'experiencing the qualities of a thing' in such a way as to find them 'worthy or valuable' (Dickie 1974: 40) or 'perceiving, cognizing, or otherwise experiencing' the work 'where such experience may involve the imagination, and on the other hand, deriving satisfaction from it or regarding it positively' (Levinson 2009: 415). And it is something like this which is often taken to be the sine qua non of our aesthetic engagement with artworks. Sibley (1965: 137) claims that 'Merely to learn from others, on good authority, that the music is serene, the play moving, or the picture unbalanced is of little aesthetic value; the crucial thing is to see, hear, or feel' (see also, e.g., Ransom 2019: 425–429).

Indeed, it hasn't just been claimed that aesthetic judgements based on the word of others lack value but that there is something illegitimate about forming our aesthetic judgements in this way. Pessimism concerning aesthetic testimony (hereafter 'pessimism') is, roughly, the position that it is illegitimate to form aesthetic judgements on the basis of testimony with the opposing position, optimism concerning aesthetic testimony (hereafter 'optimism'), being the denial of this claim. (These names were first introduced in Hopkins 2007 as labels for parallel positions in the debate surrounding moral testimony. For a fuller discussion of the nature of these competing views see Robson 2022: 18–31). The debate between the optimist and the pessimist has been the most prominent debate in recent aesthetic epistemology, and we will return to it a number of times in later sections. (Prominent defences of pessimism include Hopkins 2000, Gorodeisky 2010, and Hills 2022. Prominent defences of optimism include Meskin 2004, Laetz 2008, McKinnon 2017 and Robson 2022.)

Regardless of what we make of these debates, though, aesthetic knowledge itself doesn't seem to matter very much. If I somehow know that the film I am watching is beautiful, but am unable to personally appreciate that beauty in a rewarding way, then there seems little value to my continuing to engage with it. Section 4 briefly sets the scene by presenting the optimistic thought that we can acquire aesthetic knowledge on the basis of testimony. While I will suggest various reasons for being sympathetic to the optimist's position throughout this work, I don't intend to offer a full-fledged defence of optimism (something I've already undertaken at length in Robson 2022). Rather, the primary purpose of presenting the optimist's claim is to use it as a springboard for arguing that Claim Three is mistaken and that there are an array of ways in which aesthetic knowledge (and specifically aesthetic knowledge formed on the basis of testimony) can prove surprisingly valuable. I finish by suggesting that this conclusion helps to open up exciting new areas of research for aesthetic epistemology.

2 The Problems of Aesthetic Perception

In the previous section we briefly looked at three common views which might be taken to undermine the value of my project in this Element. In this section, we'll focus on the first of these: the thesis that perception is obviously the most reliable route to aesthetic knowledge. Before we begin, though, it's worth noting two points. First, I will talk in this section as if our aesthetic judgements are, in various respects, analogous to everyday judgements concerning, for example, shape and colour. In some ways, this hardly seems remarkable. Comparing aesthetic judgements to colour judgements is a very common and has a long history (Sibley 1965: 135, Watkins and Shelley 2012). However, in other respects, it is highly controversial, and in the next section, we will consider some suggestions that the nature of aesthetic judgement differs in crucial ways – being relative to the perceiver, being merely the expression of some non-cognitive state, and so on – from more mundane judgements. I will argue there that these debates matter surprisingly little for the matter at hand, but, for now, I will largely ignore them and will talk as if there is a straightforward fact of the matter when it comes to aesthetic issues and that the underlying semantics of aesthetic judgements don't differ from those of mundane judgements (though for some non-standard accounts of semantics in the colour case see Roberts et al. 2014 and Simpson 2020). Another putative difference is worth highlighting, though. It is very common to suggest (Pettit 1983: 25, Alcaraz León 2008: 292, Gorodeisky 2010: 55) that there is some epistemic difference between the aesthetic case and other cases. In particular, it is often suggested that – while perception is *a* route to knowledge in the case of shapes and colours – it is the *only* route to knowledge in aesthetics. I will return to this topic at length later and explain why I take this view to be mistaken.

Second, I should stress that I am by no means a general sceptic when it comes to learning about the aesthetic properties of objects via perception. As I write this, some very pretty flowers are blooming outside my office window, and I certainly accept that I can know the truth of this aesthetic claim without recourse to any evidence beyond my own perceptions. Further, even in the case of complex artworks, I don't believe that perception (even that of non-experts) is *never* a route to aesthetic knowledge. I will merely argue that it is a mistake to take it to be the most reliable route to such knowledge.

2.1 Aesthetics and Perception

I mentioned in the previous section that there are long-standing links between aesthetics and perception, and examples of this aren't difficult to find. Monroe Beardsley (1981: 46) maintains that '[t]he aesthetic object is a perceptual object'. That is, any object capable of being subject to genuine aesthetic evaluation must be one whose properties 'are open to direct sensory awareness' (Monroe Beardsley 1981: 31). In a different vein, Bence Nanay (2014: 101) argues that there are (or should be) very close methodological links between philosophical aesthetics and the philosophy of perception, maintaining that 'many, maybe even most traditional problems in aesthetics are in fact about philosophy of perception and can, as a result, be fruitfully addressed with the help of the conceptual apparatus of the philosophy of perception'. And other examples include Sibley's claim (1965:137) that 'aesthetics deals with a kind of perception', Walton's (1970: 337) claim that 'there is something right in the idea that what matters aesthetically about a painting or a sonata is just how it looks or sounds', and Pettit's claim (1983: 25) that '[a]esthetic characterisations are essentially perceptual'. Each of these claims is, of course, controversial, but they illustrate how commonly the aesthetic and the perceptual are taken to be intertwined (for some further discussions of the relationship between aesthetics and perception see Margolis (1960), Sibley (1965), Schellekens (2009), and Robson (2018)).

It is, however, surprisingly controversial whether we can even perceive aesthetic properties. We certainly talk about, say, seeing that a painting is beautiful but some philosophers will deny that this is, strictly speaking, true and there are ongoing debates about precisely which properties we can literally have perceptual experience of. As Heather Logue (2013:1) notes, '[p]retty much everyone agrees that we can visually experience something's color, shape, size, and location properties', but whether we literally see other 'higher-level' properties – such as being a penguin or being fragile – is far more controversial. And aesthetic properties clearly fall into the second, more controversial, camp. Thankfully, we need not get into these debates here (though see Sedivy 2018 and Logue 2018) since, for the most part at least, the kinds of claim about perception I am concerning myself with in this section typically use perceptual terminology in a rather broader and looser sense. To see this, consider the quote from Sibley (1965:137) again in its proper context.

> It is of importance to note first that, broadly speaking, aesthetics deals with a kind of perception. People have to *see* the grace or unity of a work, *hear* the plaintiveness or frenzy in the music, *notice* the gaudiness of a color scheme feel the power of a novel, its mood, or its uncertainty of tone. They may be struck by these qualities at once, or they may come to perceive them only after repeated viewings, hearings, or readings, and with the help of critics.

Similarly, he notes elsewhere (Sibley 1959: 423) that it 'is with an ability to notice or discern things that I am concerned'. What precisely this sense of perception amounts to is a controversial matter (see Margolis 1966), but, for now, we should just note that it's broad enough to encompass cases where we need guidance, training, and skill to perceive things as well as those – such as feeling the power of a novel – where perceptual terminology will likely need to be taken non-literally. The key thought here (see Romanos 1977, Shelley 2003) is often to distinguish the kind of immediacy, which perception in this sense has, from the use of, say, various kinds of inference. This isn't to say that our perceptual capacities cannot be trained or develop over time (Sibley 1959: 446 and others – such as Ransom 2022 and Montero 2012 – clearly believe that they can), but only that the act of perceiving itself is immediate in the relevant sense.

This last point, concerning training, is very important. I have suggested that it is common to take it to be obvious that perception is the paradigm route to aesthetic knowledge. To say that it is easy, in these general terms at least, to answer the question of how best to acquire knowledge isn't to say that it is always easy to acquire aesthetic knowledge. Of course, someone who defends Claim One could also make this further commitment but philosophically informed defenders of the claim are unlikely to do so. Rather, they will likely allow that fully perceiving the aesthetic properties of a complex artwork can often require considerable training, guidance by expert critics, and patient exploration of the work itself (see Ransom 2022). Similarly, to say that it is obvious *that* we acquire aesthetic knowledge most reliably through perception isn't to say that it is obvious *how* we acquire aesthetic knowledge via perception. As already highlighted (in §1.2), there are ongoing debates regarding how perception and perceptual knowledge (both aesthetic and otherwise) function. Further, to say that perception, in this broad sense, is obviously the most reliable basis for our aesthetic judgements isn't to say that aesthetic judgements of this kind are anything like infallible. Finally, my opponent is in no way committed to the claim that appreciation begins and ends with perception. It is common, for example, to take a certain kind of pleasurable response to play a key part in paradigm aesthetic appreciation (Matthen 2017, Gorodeisky 2021) and to take the acquisition of certain cognitive states to be a (or even *the*) central aim of aesthetic appreciation (Young 2003).

The claim my opponent is making is merely that it is easy to identify the epistemically (and likely otherwise) paradigmatic route to aesthetic knowledge as perceptual. For example, Philip Pettit (1983: 25) claims that in aesthetics 'perception is the only title to the sort of knowledge which perception yields – let us say, to the full knowledge – of the truths which they express'. Further, other influential aesthetic principles, while not explicitly framed in terms of perception, are often interpreted in this way. For example, Richard Wollheim's (1980: 233) famous acquaintance principle holds that 'judgements of aesthetic value, unlike judgements of moral knowledge, must be based on first-hand experience of their objects and are not, except within very narrow limits, transmissible from one person to another'; 'first-hand experience' here is typically – though, for dissenting interpretations see Lopes 2014b: 170 and Shelley 2023 – taken to be perceptual experience (at least in the broad sense being used here). We will return later to the question of why Wollheim et al. denigrate sources of aesthetic judgement other than direction perception. For now, though, the key point to note is how quickly claims of this kind are made. Both Wollheim and Pettit (as well as others who have followed them) take the privileged status of perception as something like a starting point, a datum to be explained, rather than a controversial thesis which needs establishing. Why, then, might anyone be sceptical of the positive epistemic status of perception in aesthetics?

One obvious reason for doubting the reliability of perception, dating back at least as far as Hume (1757 / 1875), is the widespread phenomenon of aesthetic disagreement. Disagreements over the question of whether particular works instantiate particular aesthetic properties are, of course, widespread, and it would seem that in any case where two individuals take opposing stances at least one of them must be wrong. This looks to provide the basis for a very quick argument against the reliability of aesthetic perception, but, as we will see in the next section, it isn't clear that this disagreement (or apparent disagreement) needs to be explained in a way which commits us to thinking that at least one party in the dispute is mistaken. And, given this, the move from disagreement to unreliability is (at best) more circuitous than it might initially appear. Rather than disagreement, then, my concerns focus on how challenging it is for someone to put themselves in a position to properly judge aesthetic matters (or even to judge what they themselves actually value aesthetically) on the basis of perception.

Sceptical considerations about our capacities as aesthetic judges are hardly new. Hume (1757 / 1875: 255) famously claimed that a 'true judge' in aesthetics who is able to reliably judge the aesthetic character of works is extremely rare. This is because to be a judge of this kind requires a range of qualities – such as extensive practice and comparison with a wide range of case, natural skill and discernment, and a complete absence of various biases – which are rarely found in isolation and are even less common in combination. To go into just one area of concern here, Hume (1757 / 1875: 255) focuses heavily on various kinds of prejudice and bias which can distort our aesthetic judgements, arguing that it is very rare to find anyone who allows 'nothing to enter into his consideration but the very object' being judged and that '[a]uthority or prejudice' can often give 'a temporary vogue to a bad poet or orator'. Nor are such concerns uniquely Humean. Similar concerns can be seen expressed by contemporary aestheticians such as Johnson King (2023) and Hogan (1994). This traditional scepticism goes quite far, and it certainly goes significantly further that our common sense understanding of aesthetics would often allow. However, we can go further still by considering what some empirical work has taught us about our reliability (of the lack of same) as aesthetic judges.

2.2 Empirical Concerns

An increasing range of empirical work has highlighted ways in which our firsthand aesthetic judgements are unreliable due to being strongly influenced by aesthetically irrelevant factors. That is, factors which virtually everyone would reflectively deny have any impact on the actual aesthetic qualities of the work in question. I'll consider two primary examples here: ordering effects and social factors (such as race and gender). These are merely the tip of the iceberg, but they do a good job of highlighting the nature of the concern.

In terms of ordering effects, a plethora of studies have shown that '[w]henever competing options are considered in sequence, their evaluations may be affected by order of appearance' (de Bruin 2006: 245). For example, it has been shown that the job candidates who interview first and last have a significant advantage over their rivals (Strawn and Thorsteinson 2015), and these effects also clearly arise in a range of aesthetic cases. To focus on just one example, Ginsburgh and Ours (2003: 294) argued that with respect to at least one prominent classical musical competition 'the opinion of music critics is more influenced by the ranking than by the quality of the performers'. Once again, those who performed first and last typically have an advantage (a pattern which recurs in judgements in areas as disparate as figure skating (de Bruin 2006) and Eurovision performances (Antipov and Elena 2017)).

Similarly, irrelevant social factors, such as race and gender, have repeatedly been shown to influence our aesthetic judgements (for some general discussions of race and gender in aesthetics see Taylor 2016, Eaton 2008, Perina 2009, Arguello 2019 and Korsmeyer and Weiser 2021). To use one famous example, a number of orchestras have recently introduced screens in their auditions to prevent (among other things) the gender of the performer from being known to the judging panel. Such procedures are often motivated by the concern that a lack of anonymity might disadvantage women during the audition process, and this worry appears to be justified. A series of studies by Claudia Goldin and Cecilia Rouse (2000), for example, showed that 'the screen increases – by 50 percent – the probability that a woman will be advanced from certain preliminary rounds and increases by severalfold the likelihood that a woman will be selected in the final round' (738).

Again, these are only representative examples and are part of a much wider pattern of empirical concerns (for more see Irvin 2014, Lopes 2014a, Robson 2022: 59–60, and Johnson King 2023). Further, studies have shown that our aesthetic judgements can be influenced by a whole slate of factors, ranging from mere exposure to a particular work (Cutting 2006) to the perceived price of an object (Plassmann et al. 2008). All of this certainly gives us some reason to doubt our first-hand aesthetic judgements (just how much of a reason is something I return to later), but that's not *all* that it does. Consider, for example, the old saw that someone 'doesn't know much about art but knows what they like'. The kinds of empirical consideration we have been considering appear to undermine even this limited level of confidence. We have seen, for example, that ordering effects can make a considerable difference to our aesthetic judgements, but, of course, most people don't take these to be part of what makes them like or dislike a work. Indeed, it seems plausible to suggest that, in some sense, someone who only judges work *a* to be better than work *b* due to ordering effects doesn't *really* like work *a* more (I return to this point in §3.2).

2.3 Responding to These Empirical Worries

The next question to ask is how someone might aim to respond to these sceptical concerns. Before we begin, though, it's worth repeating my earlier point that I'm only suggesting that these empirical worries support a rather attenuated version of scepticism regarding aesthetic perception. That is, they don't show that perception of this kind *can't* provide knowledge, but only that it is much less reliable at doing so than has often been presupposed. If this is true, then a defender of Claim One would need to show that it is obvious that no other method for acquiring aesthetic knowledge can meet, or exceed, even this lower standard. In order to perform such a task, they'd likely need to either show that all rival routes to knowledge are clearly even more beset by difficulties than perception or else argue that it is easy to rule out any other putative rival as even *being* another route to aesthetic knowledge. I will argue later that neither of these tasks looks very promising. For now, though, let's consider how someone might try to defend the epistemic status of perception itself.

A first line of response is to deny that these concerns actually apply to aesthetic judgements at all. A lot of empirical work of the kind I've discussed has tended to focus on prompts which ask about the subjects 'likings' or 'preferences', rather than on aesthetic judgements as such. Of course, there are likely to be considerable areas of overlap between the two (since people have a tendency to, e.g., like the objects they find beautiful) but to merely express a liking for something isn't yet to report any aesthetic judgement. Indeed, we will see some further arguments for the importance of separating the two in (§3.2). This is true so far as it goes, but there are certainly limits to this form of defence. First, some of these worries have been shown to arise for a wide range of different prompts (beyond mere preferences and likings). The mere exposure effect, for example, has (as discussed in Zajonc 1968 and Bornstein 1989) consistently been shown to arise with respect to a vast range of measures. Second, and more generally, as Meskin et al. (2013: 140) point out there tends to be a high degree of consistency amongst various measures in experimental work of this kind. Given this, the fact that some irrelevant factors influence our reports of what we like is strong prima facie reason to think that we would find the same pattern with regard to aesthetic judgement. At the very least, the burden of proof seems to be on the person looking to deny the inference here.

A further line of response is to argue that, while these distorting factors have a significant influence on the judgements of ordinary appreciators, they don't undermine the judgements of experts. If this is correct, then these empirical concerns will help to add emphasis to the traditional Humean scepticism – according to which reliable aesthetic judgement is the purview of a very few true judges – but won't move us significantly beyond it. Before responding to this concern, though, it's worth noting that, even if we don't go beyond the more traditional forms of scepticism, this would still concede that there are significant issues with *our* ability to reliably judge the aesthetic value of works via perception. I'm certainly no Humean true judge, and I suspect that very few of my readers are either (if you are, then I hope you also have the moral virtue of forgiveness in addition to all of your aesthetic ones). And, as I will contend in §4.2, none of us are genuine experts when it comes to *all* (or even the majority) of the different artforms in the world. Is it true that expert judges perform better in the relevant ways though? With respect to some instances of ordering effects, Haan et al. (2005: 72) found that 'experts are unambiguously better judges of quality' in terms of being less susceptible to such effects (for similar conclusions concerning other distorting factors see Carlson and Bond 2006). These studies aren't unambiguously good news, though, as they don't show anything like an expert immunity to these distorting factors, but merely that they're less susceptible to them than the rest of us. And there's even worse news elsewhere, with other studies showing that experts perform no better, and sometimes even less well, than others (see Sen 1998 and cf. Ashton (2012) on concerns about the reliability of expert wine tasters).

Finally, someone might accept that these distorting factors are genuine, and genuinely problematic, but propose taking efforts to ameliorate their effects, and a number of philosophers have suggested methods for doing so. Sherri Irvin (2014: 52), for example, agrees that our ability to introspect the reasons for our aesthetic judgements is 'seriously called into question' by the kinds of empirical work we have been discussing. However, she suggests (Irvin 2014: 52) that this problem can be ameliorated by replacing a reliance on introspection of one's aesthetic judgements with merely introspectively accessing 'the flow of one's occurrent perceptual, cognitive and emotional *states*, combined with accurate theoretical knowledge about causal relations between aspects of a work and people's responses'. The first of these she suggests might be assisted by various mindfulness techniques Irvin 2014, 48–9), the second by increased knowledge of empirical work in aesthetics (Irvin 2014, 53). However, even if such techniques are effective (and this is far from having been established), they seem to promise only to reduce the negative impacts of distorting effects rather than eliminating them altogether.

2.4 The Test of Time

I have suggested, then, that there is good reason to be sceptical when it comes to the reliability of many of our first-hand aesthetic judgements and even of our attempts to identify what it is that we ourselves like or value in particular works. I don't mean to suggest that these considerations should lead to a complete scepticism about first-hand aesthetic judgement – and some of the responses discussed in the previous section might go some way towards mitigating the concerns – but I do maintain that they give us significant reason to hold that we (both the folk and philosophically inclined aestheticians) have tended to overvalue perception when it comes to aesthetic knowledge. Is there a rival route, though, that can undermine claims to the obvious epistemic superiority of perception? I believe that there is.

My answer here is, again, inspired by Hume, who argues that the surest test of the aesthetic value of an artwork is whether its reputation is able to survive 'changes of climate, government, religion, and language' (Hume 1757 / 1875: 255). That is, whether it passes what has come to be known as 'the test of time'. A test of this kind also has a range of contemporary proponents including Anita Silvers (1991: 211), who suggests that an artwork cannot attain 'canonical status totally independently of its ability to inspire enduring aesthetic admiration', and Jerrold Levinson (2002: 233), who argues that if works excel at this test, then it is 'a reasonable supposition that such works have a high artistic value' (for an extended explication and defence of the test of time see Savile 1982). I've talked about *the* test of time but it isn't always obvious that there's a single test in play, with each of the writers cited differing on some important details. The key idea, though, is that a strong level of support can be adduced for an aesthetic judgement by learning that this judgement is widely shared not only by contemporary critics but also by a consensus of critics across different times and cultures (despite the name, those who invoke the test of time frequently also appeal to synchronic consensus, since we can encounter variations in 'climate, government, religion, and language' by moving geographically as well as chronologically).

A few points are worth noting here. First, it is important to clarify that the version of the test of time I am proposing is the one which I take to be best able to help us in responding to the kinds of sceptical worries I have discussed in this section. There are likely some elements of this version of the test which Hume (and other influential defenders of tests of this kind) would disagree with. However, while I will draw on some elements of their work, my purpose here is an epistemic (rather than exegetical) one. Second, I have deliberately made appeal to critics here and will take it for granted that critics will tend to have some significant degree of expertise in their area(s) of operation (see Carroll 2009). I don't mean to suggest that very many (if any) of these critics will be Humean true judges though and, as was discussed earlier, there's good reason to think that even experts will find themselves susceptible to at least some of the distorting factors we've looked at. Third, 'consensus' here shouldn't be understood as literally requiring complete unanimity. Even restricting ourselves to our own time and culture, there will always be outliers arguing that some critical darling is vastly overrated (one outrageous recent review even dared to criticise *Paddington 2*, ruining its perfect Rotten Tomatoes score). This becomes even more obvious when we widen our view. As Hume himself notes, various factors can give 'a temporary vogue to a bad poet or orator' (1757 / 1875: 255), and, as we will discuss later, this will often lead to a work being heavily praised by critics in its own time but then savaged or neglected by later critics. The reverse also sometimes famously happens, but these cases tend to be the exception since works not applauded in their own time are very often quickly forgotten and never even become candidates for critical reappraisal. In the case of such forgotten works, the version of the test I'm proposing is simply silent on their value (rather than taking them to have failed the test). Finally, I am not meaning to suggest that the version test of time I propose achieves (or even approximates) infallibility. I believe that it is our most secure route to aesthetic knowledge, and that it avoids many pitfalls to which first-hand aesthetic perception often succumbs, but this doesn't mean that it never errs.

Let us imagine, then, that we are faced with some particular work which passes the test of time. Why am I suggesting that this will provide us with more secure knowledge than (even an expert) judging the work on the basis of first-hand perception? We have seen that a test of this kind has considerable support – both historical and contemporary – but how does it help us with our current concerns? To answer this question, let's start by considering Sibley's (1968: 50–51) claim that the

> possibility of error with a case that has elicited long-lasting convergence decreases as possible explanations of error become more obviously absurd; e.g. we could not sensibly reject a centuries-spanning consensus about *Oedipus* as being the result of personal bias, enthusiasm for a novel style, or passing fashions or fads. I do not mean that, in other cases, there is always some reason for doubt; only that the long-attested cases may virtually exclude the theoretical sceptic's doubt as absurd.

The kinds of biases and similar that have traditionally been proposed in aesthetics come in various forms, and Sibley's points may not be applicable to all of them (for example, snobbery is a ubiquitous aesthetic concern (see Patridge

2023) and, once a work has acquired a certain status, snobbery may help to cement this for future critics). But the examples of bias Sibley mentions are fairly straightforwardly overcome by appealing to the test of time. None of us, I assume, have any personal axes to grind with Sophocles, nor do we have any personal investment in the fates of the various states he represents in his work (and the same will apply to the vast majority of critics who have discussed his work in the many centuries since its writing). Similarly, I don't think much needs to be said to refute the claim that *Oedipus*' current reputation rests on any appeal to novelty or mercurial fashion.

Can something similar be said about the empirical worries I have considered? I believe it can. The order that a work is seen in will, for example, vary depending on the viewer, as will other irrelevant factors which might influence how they view the work. And, of course, if we are more sanguine about the prospects for expert judgements than those of laypeople, then so much the better for the test. It might be objected, though, that the test of time doesn't eliminate, and indeed can help to reinforce, the kinds of problematic social factors I've discussed earlier. As various discussions have noted (e.g., Citron 1990, Barzman 1994 and Lauter 2013), those works considered canonical have often tended to be created by a very narrow group of socially privileged individuals with, for example, art by women and people of colour often being excluded. Given this, it's worth thinking further about how we should interpret the test of time in relation to the canon. In terms of being omitted from the canon, many works will fail to be included, not because they are consistently judged poorly but merely because they are forgotten. And being the work of an individual who belongs to some group that is marginalised or oppressed in some significant way is, of course, likely to greatly increase the odds of this happening. As indicated earlier, though, the version of the test I propose is silent on such works. It is not that a critical consensus has taken any stance on these works, but, rather, it has merely been failed to render any verdict on them. This is not, of course, to suggest that we should regard the exclusion of works by marginalised authors as unproblematic, far from it. Rather, the point is merely that these deep injustices aren't directly relevant to assessing the reliability of the test of time as I am interpreting it. That said, I should repeat my earlier point that I don't mean to suggest that the test of time is infallible and there likely will be cases where sufficiently entrenched and long-standing prejudices do lead to 'false negatives'. Consider, for example, cases where a work by a marginalised artist is well-regarded enough to be preserved for critical attention but where persistent and entrenched prejudices still lead to it being consistently undervalued compared to comparable work by more privileged artists (thanks to an anonymous referee for suggesting cases of this kind).

2.5 The Sources of Aesthetic Knowledge

In this section, I have been arguing that perception isn't the best route to aesthetic knowledge and so, *a fortiori*, isn't (contra Claim One) *obviously* the best route to aesthetic knowledge. I have done this by arguing that perception as a route to aesthetic knowledge encounters some significant challenges which an alternative path to aesthetic knowledge, appeals to the test of time, does not. How, though, do we learn from the test of time? That is, if the source of knowledge here isn't perceptual, then what is it? A large part of the test of time is likely to be testimonial. This might seem a strange claim to make since it's clear that we will have never talked with most (perhaps all) of the critics whose judgements the test of time appeals to. However, in the contemporary philosophical literature 'testimony' is used in a broader sense, and, as Sosa (1991: 219) puts, things 'requires only that it be a statement of someone's thoughts or beliefs, which they might direct to the world at large and to no one in particular' (for more on this broad notion of testimony see Lackey 2006: 433). Further, as discussed in (Coady 1992: 199–223), this testimony need not be first-hand – from the critics themselves – and those of us without much interest in reading historical art criticism can still learn from this testimony at second, third, or nth remove. It is clear, then, that a significant part of the test of time will involve deference to testimony but, as McGrath (2009) highlights, there are various forms of deference beyond deferring to someone else's word via testimony. For example, we might defer to someone's judgements about which restaurant in a town to dine at by asking their opinion, but we can also do so merely by observing which restaurants they themselves regularly frequent.

My claim that this kind of deference – both testimonial and more broadly – is (given the right circumstances) a better source of aesthetic knowledge than perception is likely to be a rather surprising one. Indeed, it isn't just that perception has often been taken to be the best route to aesthetic knowledge but that it has sometimes been taken to be the *only* route to such knowledge. On such a view, the question of how best to get aesthetic knowledge would, of course, be incredibly easy to answer. Perception, whatever challenges it may face, simply wins by default. Pettit (1983: 25), for example, maintains that in most areas 'perception and testimony may count as titles to the full knowledge of the truth which that sentence expresses' but that perception is the only route to 'full knowledge' in aesthetics. And similar ideas can be found in, for example, Wollheim's acquaintance principle discussed earlier (as well as earlier ideas expressed in, e.g., Mothersill 1961 and Tormey 1973). Of course, interpretation here is a difficult matter, and it's not immediately obvious that all of these claims are intended to be epistemic. For example, Lopes (2014b: 170) has recently argued (mistakenly in my view, see Wallbank and Robson 2022) that 'the controversy over the acquaintance principle ensues from an incorrect interpretation of it'. According to Lopes (2014b: 175), we shouldn't interpret the acquaintance principle as a claim about acquiring aesthetic *knowledge* (for other non-epistemic readings of the principle see, e.g., Shelly 2023) but about the appropriate circumstances for a particular kind of appreciation. Still, as with the quote from Pettit, some claims of this kind – including, as Lopes highlights, the vast majority of interpretations of the acquaintance principle – are explicitly epistemic, and even some of Wollheim's own discussion makes reference to 'experience as an epistemic condition of aesthetic evaluation' (1980: 233).

Even once we settle on whether to interpret these claims epistemically, though, there is some debate about precisely which sources of aesthetic judgement are taken to be ruled out (and ruled in) here. A standard line allows perception (in the broad sense under consideration here) of the object itself, but also allows experience of close replicas, photographs and so on of that object (for debates about what to admit here see Livingston 2003 and Robson 2013). Even broader accounts may, as Hopkins (2006: 93–4) suggests, allow for sensory imagination to also be legitimised. Others focus less on acquaintance with the object and more on acquaintance with certain kinds of aesthetic property (Lord 2018). Still, it seems clear that several candidate sources of knowledge are intended to be ruled out. Probably the most prevalent source of aesthetic judgement taken to be ruled out by such principle is inferences based on so-called 'principles of taste'. That is, we should – as Kant (1790/2005: 95) famously argued – reject any appeal in aesthetics to 'a principle under the condition of which we could subsume the concept of an object and thus infer by means of a syllogism that the object is beautiful'. This is often taken to mean that there is no (non-aesthetic) feature of a work which we can reliably point to in order to infer that it is beautiful. And subsequent discussion has broadened this to deny that we can infer the presence of any aesthetic property in this way. (Though, as Sibley (1965: 153) notes, it seems uncontroversial that we can infer their absence. A huge sphere of solid steel will certainly fail to be dainty.)

Subsequent discussions of principles of taste, and similar kinds of inference, remained a prominent part of aesthetics for quite some time, but it is rare to find any contemporary defenders of the kind of inference Kant rejects. (Some key contributions to this debate include Isenberg (1949), Kennick (1958), Sibley (1959), Hungerland (1968), Dickie (1987), and Davies 1990)). For a more recent exegetical take on the debate see Bergqvist (2010).) Perhaps the biggest exception here concerns some of the more ambitious work in neuroaesthetics where it is sometimes suggested, on the basis of empirical work on the brain, that we can infer aesthetic properties from features of a work or our reactions to it. Consider for, example, Calvo-Merino et al.'s (2008: 920) conclusion that

> We found that the degree of whole-body movement is a major driver of aesthetic evaluation of dance, and also has reliable consensus correlates in sensorimotor and visual form processing areas of the human brain. Therefore, our results give rise to the possibility of a 'menu' of dance moves, from which artists could choose those which target aesthetically sensitive areas.

Here, they seem to suggest that their work has highlighted a clear link between positive aesthetic evaluation of dance performance and the degree of whole-body movement. It is worth noting, though, that they are (as with other neuro-aestheticians) sometimes significantly more guarded and nuanced in their defence of such principles than some of their critics – and some of their own bolder pronouncements – might suggest (see Davies 2014: 57–74 for some discussion of this and other relevant work along with the important caveats neuro-aestheticians themselves introduce).

There are, however, defenders of weaker versions of these principles, with Monroe Beardsley (1962) arguing that there are certain features – as well as 'pairs and clusters of features' (484) – which always serve to make a work better (and other features which always tend to make it worse). He argues that this would allow us to infer of a work, from the fact that it possesses one of these properties, that it is aesthetically better (or worse) than it would have been otherwise. Others reject even these diluted appeals to critical principles. Mary Mothersill (1961: 75), for example, maintains that there 'is *no* characteristic which is amenable to independent explanation and which by its presence enhances the aesthetic value' of a work (or of any sub-class of works).

While principles of taste are widely discussed, they aren't the only kind of inference we might want to make in the aesthetic case, and defenders of these principles would likely want to rule out the full range of such inferences (including, for example, enumerative induction from past cases). As well as inference, these principles are also generally taken to rule out knowledge by testimony and (I assume, though this is rarely made explicit) by appeal to other forms of deference. Further, even leaving aside these broader principles, testimony itself has often been singled out as being inadmissible when it comes to aesthetic judgement. Indeed, Kant himself (1790 / 2005: 94) seems to specifically rule out testimony as a source of aesthetic judgement, and this negative view of aesthetic testimony is explicitly advanced by later pessimists. Again, though, it isn't clear that these claims need to be read epistemically. Indeed, some of the most prominent recent defenders of views of this kind have explicitly rejected the claim that the problem with testimony in aesthetics is its inability to provide us with knowledge. The suggestion is instead that the concern is with testimony's being unable to foster other goods such as understanding 'the *aesthetic* grounds' for the judgement (Hopkins 2011: 149) or that it doesn't allow us to fully develop our aesthetic virtues (Ransom 2019) or display an appropriate level of autonomy (Nguyen 2020). I will return to these other avenues of criticism in §4.3. Why do I take this widespread scepticism about non-perceptual sources of aesthetic judgement to be mistaken? A complete defence of this would take a book in itself – indeed it took Robson (2022) – but I hope to give some indication in §4.2 as to why I take a position of this kind to be less convincing than others have argued. For now, though, I will simply note that I have already given reason to take at least one kind of deference – that involving the test of time – to be a promising source of aesthetic knowledge. Those who wish to deny this will need to provide positive reasons for doing so. As I have indicated earlier, pessimism is sometimes taken for granted rather than regarded as a controversial thesis to be argued for. It was once very common to see pessimism concerning aesthetic testimony either assumed as part of a larger argument (Matravers 2005: 198–200, Schellekens 2007: 117) or treated as something like a datum to be explained (Hopkins 2000, Goldman 2006: 333). Things have started to shift here lately, though, and (at the very least) I hope that the considerations I have adduced earlier – and those I will offer in §4.2 – will provide readers with reason to doubt that we should so easily take pessimism for granted. For now, though, I want to turn to a second concern for the project of investigating aesthetic knowledge.

3 Disputing about Taste

In this section we're going to look at some reasons for thinking that appealing to aesthetic knowledge must be either trivial or impossible. Elisabeth Schellekens (2009: 734) frames the challenge faced by those of us working on issues of taste (aesthetic and otherwise) as follows; 'given that one of the few generally admitted principles concerning taste lies precisely in the observation that there can be no universal agreement, it would be easy to conclude that there is nothing, in fact, to be held up for general philosophical examination'. This concern is perhaps most prominent when it comes to considering the issues of (apparent) aesthetic disagreement. This presents us with a difficult starting point, though, since the combination of attitudes which people often seem inclined to adopt towards aesthetic disagreement is a strange one. Andy Egan (2010: 247) captures this strangeness very well.

> 'There's no disputing about taste'. That's got a nice ring to it, but it's not quite the ring of truth. While there's definitely something right about the

> aphorism – there's a reason why it ... tends to produce so much nodding of heads and muttering of 'just so' and 'yes, quite' –... One thing that's pretty clear is that what's right about the aphorism, that there's no disputing about taste, isn't that there's no disputing about taste ... it takes great care and good aim to fling a brick without hitting somebody who's engaged in a dispute about taste.

Egan here is highlighting competing aspects of our aesthetic practice which, to say the least, don't fit neatly together. The idea that aesthetic judgements are somehow subjective or 'mere matters of taste' is one that many will find appealing (Cova et al. 2019 offer some empirical evidence for this). Further, claims of this kind can easily be taken to support the famous maxim that 'there's no disputing about taste'. Yet, as Egan highlights, this claim (if taken as a descriptive one) is clearly false and conflicts with a second aspect of our aesthetic practice. Even a casual scan of webpages devoted to films or music will uncover scores of people debating the aesthetic merits (or lack of same) of various works. Indeed, far from being an area where there is unusually little disputation, aesthetic matters seem to rank alongside the likes of politics and sports as one of the topics which people are most inclined to spend their time debating. Of course, as Egan notes, the aphorism is rarely taken to deny that people do sometimes disagree about matters of taste (though, as we'll see later, some views of aesthetic dispute do make this rather hard to capture) but, rather, to make some normative claim about the value or appropriateness of doing so. Still, this hardly makes our predicament less strange. If we are all so convinced that there is no value to debating matters of taste, then why do we spend so much of our time doing so?

In this section, I will look at this question and what it might teach us about aesthetic knowledge. While there is much that could be said in response to these challenges, I will focus on the common idea that there is a certain kind of disagreement – so called 'faultless disagreement' – which is hard to square with positions which take there to be a straightforward 'fact of the matter' in aesthetics. I will then survey some alternative positions – such as subjectivism and expressivism – which might be taken to do a better job here. We will see that it is controversial whether these views really can do any better at accommodating intuitions of faultlessness. Regardless, though, I will argue that the most plausible versions of these views allow for there to be substantive questions of aesthetic knowledge worthy of sustained investigation. Further, I will also suggest that such views are amenable to the idea of expertise and to the views about the importance of the social in aesthetic epistemology which I defended in the previous section.

Before looking at arguments against the possibility of substantive knowledge, though, it is important to say a little more about what it would mean to have (or to fail to have) aesthetic knowledge which is substantive in the relevant sense. First, and most obviously, we could fail to have substantive aesthetic knowledge by virtue of failing to have aesthetic knowledge at all. For example, we might think that, on certain of the views I will discuss in this section, if the question concerns what is *really* beautiful or ugly or graceful or ..., then knowledge of this kind would be impossible. On these views, the thought goes, there simply are no aesthetic truths of, and therefore no prospects for aesthetic knowledge of, this kind. Second, there are cases where we might allow that we can have aesthetic knowledge but take this to lack some property which would makes it a worthy object of serious and sustained epistemic investigation (this being what I mean by such knowledge failing to be 'substantive' in the relevant sense). We might think, for example, that if we are merely asking for truth of what is, say, 'beautiful for me', then we can arrive at knowledge of this matter (though we will see later that even this is controversial), but doing so is too trivial to be worthy of serious investigation. I am, after all, simply reporting my own preferences, and preferences aren't the kind of thing which is susceptible to appeal to reasons, subject to argumentative justification, and so forth. The question of whether a work is aesthetically valuable *for me* is no more worthy of serious study than the question of what my favourite pizza is (pepperoni, in case you're wondering). In what follows, I will argue that philosophical prominent 'anti-realist' views in aesthetics – such as subjectivism, relativism, and expressivism – don't require us to grasp either horn of this apparent dilemma.

3.1 Aesthetic Judgement and Disagreement

It's very common to find examples of folk discussion suggesting that some aesthetic matter isn't an appropriate object of (serious sustained) dispute since there is no 'objective' fact of the matter, and the issue is a 'subjective' or 'relative' one. However, talk about aesthetic judgements being relative, subjective, objective and so forth is likely to (and, indeed, frequently does) quickly lead to confusion unless we are a little clearer about what these notoriously slippery terms might mean. To claim that I have a headache, for example, is clearly subjective in at least one sense – that is, its depending on the mental states of some individual(s) – but it certainly isn't subjective in the sense of being 'just a matter of opinion'. Similarly, confusion can arise when we consider the common view that aesthetic judgement is very closely linked to pleasure. Kant famously held that aesthetic judgement depended on a certain kind of pleasure (1790 / 2012: 20). However, he also noted that – in contrast to differences in whether we enjoy, say, drinking Pepsi or riding rollercoasters (not

Kant's own examples of course) – aesthetic judgements possess a certain universality in that we demand 'universal agreement' (1790 / 2012: 36) when it comes to our judgements of which objects we take aesthetic pleasure in and insist on their 'validity for everyone' (1790 / 2012: 37). As in many other cases, Kant's discussion here has proven highly influential. Indeed, the majority of subsequent discussion on these issues can be seen as attempts to explain, or explain away, the tension Kant highlights.

I mentioned in the previous section that I would talk as if aesthetic discussions were very closely parallel to ordinary discourse concerning shapes and colours. This suggests that there is a single fact of the matter, discussion of these issues involves straightforward assertions of belief, knowledge is possible in these areas, and so on. One reason why people might find this kind of view unappealing is that there is widespread disagreement about aesthetic matters. How can I insist I am *objectively* right that *Holy Grail* is the best Monty Python film when I know that so many others believe that it's *Life of Brian*? By itself, though, this is hardly persuasive. A great many people believe that vaccines contain tracking microchips and that everyone before Columbus thought the Earth was flat. These people are simply mistaken, though, and their dissent should hardly cause me to doubt my own views (let alone to hold these issues to be merely matters of opinion). The real issue, then, doesn't seem to concern disagreement as such but, rather, a certain *kind* of disagreement, one which is typically labelled 'faultless disagreement'. The thought here being, roughly, that, in certain cases at least, two people can assert apparently contrary aesthetic claims without either making a mistake. We might think, for example, of a case where one expert claims '*Starry Night* is more beautiful than *The Birth of Venus*' and an opposing expert retorts that '*The Birth of Venus* is more beautiful than *Starry Night*'.

What does it mean to say that neither is at fault though? In order to address this, let's introduce a first view of the semantics of aesthetic judgement which is often termed absolutism but also sometimes referred to as realism or objectivism. (Even within philosophical aesthetics, though, the use of these terms isn't consistent and differing interpretations from the one I present can be found in, e.g., Goldman 1993, Schellekens 2008 and Young 2009.) Baker and Robson (2017: 431) define absolutism in relation to two key claims

CONTENT-VARIANCE: Aesthetic judgements are context-sensitive; that is, an aesthetic judgement may denote different propositions in different contexts of use.

TRUTH-RELATIVITY: The truth-values of aesthetic judgements may vary between contexts [of evaluation].

While some rival views accept one (or both) of these claims, the absolutist rejects them. They hold that a sentence such as '*Starry Night* is beautiful' expresses the same proposition in the mouth of anyone who utters it (that is, regardless of the 'context of use') and that the 'context of evaluation', that is 'a situation in which a (past, present, or future, actual or merely possible) utterance of a sentence might be assessed for truth or falsity' (MacFarlane 2005: 18) won't make a difference to whether the proposition expressed is true.

What should the absolutist make of aesthetic disagreement? They can certainly allow that such disagreements can be faultless in some sense. That is, they can allow that neither person made a mistake in their reasoning, that both responded appropriately to the evidence available to them and so on. As Schafer (2011: 266) puts things, the absolutist can argue that once the relevant kind of faultlessness 'is properly understood, it can be seen to be primarily epistemic in character'. Let's call this 'epistemic faultlessness'. Epistemic faultlessness seems a very familiar phenomenon and one which isn't restricted to the aesthetic realm (nor to other 'problem cases' such as matters of personal taste which I discuss later). Two detectives could reason perfectly from the evidence that each has available to them and come to entirely opposing conclusions regarding the guilt of the accused butler (whether they should revise their judgements when they learn of the other's opposing conclusion is a further issue I return to in §3.5). And, more controversially, some have argued that it is possible for two people who reason flawlessly from the *very same* evidence to end up with different credences towards a particular claim (Douven 2009). Still, the absolutist's opponents often seek to argue that our intuition is not just that aesthetic disagreements are epistemically faultless but that they are faultless in some deeper sense. It's not merely that those who've reached the wrong conclusion did so without making any error in reasoning but, rather, that the judgements themselves are free from error as well. For example, Palmira (2015: 360) claims that the faultlessness intuition 'requires us to account for faultlessness at the level of the believed propositions quite independently of how we formed the beliefs in those propositions'. This is something which the subjectivist about aesthetic judgement typically takes themselves to be able to explain.

3.2 Aesthetic Subjectivism

According to the subjectivist, the absolutist is wrong to reject CONTENT-VARIANCE and aesthetic statements really can express different propositions in the mouths of different people. Let's start with a simple form of this view. According to this view, when I say that '*Starry Night* is beautiful', there is some hidden indexical here such that the proposition I'm ultimately expressing turns out to be something like '*Starry Night* is beautiful *for me*'. Proponents of this view often take aesthetic judgements to very closely parallel so-called judgements of personal taste concerning what is, say, fun or tasty. A subjectivist of this stripe can very easily account for the faultlessness of faultless disagreement. I can truly judge that *Starry Night* is beautiful for me while, at the same time, you can truly judge that it is not beautiful for you. And, of course, we can also add that neither of us made any kind of epistemic error on our road to reaching these judgements. That is, they can allow that our apparent disagreement is faultless in every sense. What is harder is for them to account for its being a genuine disagreement. On this form of subjectivism, we no more disagree here than when one person says 'I am forty' and another 'I am not forty'. Concerns about whether the subjectivist can account for genuine disagreement have been discussed at length in the literature by subjectivists and their rivals (see Kölbel 2004, Kompa 2015 and Köhler 2012), and I will not retread them here. My concern in this section isn't to reject, or to endorse, any particular account of the nature of aesthetic judgement. Rather, my primary aim is to show that such debates have surprisingly little impact on the key epistemic claims I'm arguing for in this work. To see why this is, let's think about a slightly different concern for the subjectivist view.

The challenge for the subjectivist is not merely to account for the appearance of disagreement here but also the appearance of *reasonable* disagreement. If I say 'strawberries are tasty' and you say 'strawberries are not tasty' then it seems as if – with the possible exception of my checking a few facts I will discuss later concerning the circumstances of your strawberry eating – there is little more that could reasonably be said on the subject. Of course, some aesthetic disagreements do seem to be of this kind. It's hard, for example, to see how the conversation could usefully proceed in a debate over whether a particular shade of light blue was pretty. However, this doesn't seem to be the way in which we treat many aesthetic debates. In particular, when we are debating the merits of various complex artworks, we're very prone to offering various reasons in support of our claims and in opposition to those of our opponents (see Dorsch 2017 and Gorodesiky 2022). The concern here is not with these disagreements failing to be faultless but, rather, with their appearing to be pointless. Of course, the subjectivist could just allow that our practice of debating these issues is fundamentally confused, but this doesn't seem an attractive option for a number of reasons. To see why, let's consider this simple version of subjectivism in more detail.

What does it mean for something to be beautiful (or ugly or elegant or . . .) *for me*? One natural thought is just that I find the object beautiful. That is, roughly, that an object has a particular aesthetic property *for me* if and only if I judge it – most likely on the basis of my own first-hand assessment – to have that property. Still, a view of this kind doesn't seem very plausible. Compare this again to judgements of what is tasty. Perhaps I believe that strawberries aren't tasty because I have only ever eaten rotten strawberries or only ever eaten them immediately after brushing my teeth. In this case, even a subjectivist would likely allow that I am simply mistaken in my application of my own standards. And similar things will, of course, apply to aesthetic judgements of artworks. If I believe that *The Marriage of Figaro* is terrible because I've only ever attended incompetent performances of the work, then it doesn't appear that I'm even licensed to take the opera to be terrible *for me*. The analogy does break down rather quickly though. Imagine that I've tried a full range of strawberries in a full range of conditions and still find them to be non-tasty. What could an insistent strawberry-loving friend do here? If we were talking about some subtle flavour in a vintage wine that I was missing then, perhaps, they could suggest that my sense of (gustatory) taste is just lacking or that it is need of further training. This hardly seems plausible in this case, though, since the deliciousness that most people find in strawberries is hardly one which they take to be elusive or only open to the properly enculturated. Similarly, it would seem bizarre for them to try to change my mind by, for example, pointing out that I enjoy other fruits which are relevantly similar, describing the particular properties of strawberries which make them so delicious or pointing to surveys regarding how many people enjoy eating them. The subjectivist might say the same with respect to our engagement with artworks but they need not.

Further, there seems to be good reason to think that they *should* not. Recall, again, our practice of giving reasons in the aesthetic case (for more on this practice see Ransom 2022). The subjectivist could, of course, bite the bullet and take such practices to simply be misguided, but it is typically taken as a key desideratum in aesthetics to respect ordinary practice where possible. Indeed, we have seen that this desire to respect folk practice is often taken to be a reason for rejecting absolutist views in the first place. Similarly, recall again the various biases and distorting factors we considered in §2.2. It would certainly be very strange to insist that, say, seeing a painting multiple times makes it any more beautiful and hardly less so to say that it made it more beautiful *for me*. Thankfully for the subjectivist, there are a range of ways to spell out the thought that something is beautiful for me which aren't simply a matter of my happening to find it beautiful, but which still tie aesthetic judgements closely to my own aesthetic sensibilities. Perhaps the most prominent version of this strategy involves appealing to something like an idealised version of my reactions. Something is beautiful for me if a version of me who was free from bias, engaged with it appropriate circumstances and so forth found it to be so. Of course, even if we accept this general approach, there are a range of important questions about how best to spell out the details (for discussion of various kinds of idealisation, as well as other response dependent positions, both subjectivist and otherwise see King 2023).

While these issues are certainly worthy of investigation in their own right, they have surprisingly little impact on the conclusions I have drawn in the previous section. For my purposes, the relevant point isn't about how we answer these difficult epistemic questions but, rather, the fact that such questions exist at all. It is easy, when we talk about aesthetic judgements being subjective, to imagine a world where everyone is merely reporting their own preference which are merely arbitrary occurrences and will overlap with preferences of others, if at all, merely by coincidence. We have seen earlier, though, that this picture is an implausible one in multiple respects. Given this, it seems that we have reason to be suspicious of the claims that – even on a subjectivist view – aesthetic knowledge is either a trivial matter or is somehow rendered impossible by there being no relevant standards for appropriate judgement. Rather, (on any plausible version of the subjectivist view) our claims to knowledge will still be ones which could be mistaken and could be usefully challenged by an opponent in various ways. Further, I will also suggest in §3.4 that some of the caveats introduced earlier will allow the subjectivist (and other rival views) to retain all of the crucial aspects of the views I am defending in this work. First, though, we should say a little more about the subjectivist's rivals.

3.3 Other Rival Views

I have looked at length at the subjectivist position, but it's worth noting that subjectivism isn't the only rival to absolutism when it comes to the semantics of aesthetic judgements. Other accounts include relativism (Kölbel 2009), which rejects CONTENT-VARIANCE but accepts TRUTH-RELATIVIM, and pluralism (Miščević 2018), which maintains that 'the sentences in question can, and often do, express different judgments in the mouths of different' people (386). That is, that the semantics of one person's aesthetic judgements might be absolutist and another's, say, subjectivist. I will not, however, be exploring these positions here. This is not because I take such views to be uninteresting, far from it, but merely because I believe that the relevant claims made in this section concerning subjectivism can easily be applied, mutatis mutandis, to these views as well. There are, of course, important debates about which versions of these claims are most plausible but, as noted earlier, my aim here isn't to offer a general evaluation of any of these views. I do, however, believe that there is something to be learned from saying a little more about one further rival semantics, expressivism.

According to the expressivist about a particular domain, 'the linguistic function of the target discourse' (that is, the discourse in the domain in question) is to 'express non-belief-like mental states or "attitudes"' (Sinclair 2009: 136). This contrasts with both the absolutist and the subjectivist, who each takes our aesthetic discourse to be expressing a certain kind of belief. Expressivism remains relatively unexplored in aesthetics, especially in comparison to the extensive attention it has received in ethics, but a number of different expressivist views have still been defended (see, e.g., Scuton 1976, Todd 2004 and Marques 2016). These are views which, amongst other things, disagree about which attitudes we should take aesthetic discourse to express. Let's begin with a classic aesthetic expressivist view briefly discussed by A.J. Ayer. On Ayer's (1936: 113) view, aesthetic words 'are employed, as ethical words are employed, not to make statements of fact, but simply to express certain feelings and evoke a certain response.' To call an object 'beautiful', for example, is simply to express a certain kind of feeling of satisfaction towards it (just as we would be saying 'wow' in a certain tone or staring at the object in rapt admiration). A more recent view, put forward by Gibbard (1992: 52), maintains that aesthetic discourse expresses the acceptance of aesthetic norms where these 'are norms for the rationality of kinds of aesthetic appreciation'. To accept a norm involves, inter alia, a tendency to speak and act in accordance with the norm, to encourage others to follow the norm and to defend the norm in debate (Gibbard 1990: 71–80).

What should the expressivist say in relation to disagreement? This general issue has been explored at length in various places (see, e.g., Golub 2017, Eriksson 2016 and Merli 2008), but we'll focus here on a particular concern that has been raised for expressivism in aesthetics. It has sometimes been suggested, by both critics and proponents, that aesthetic exppressivism isn't able to capture the notion of aesthetic knowledge or even allow that aesthetic claims express propositions at all. Ayer (1936: 114) certainly takes this view and argues that 'the purpose of aesthetic criticism is not so much to give knowledge as to communicate emotion' and that, when someone discusses aesthetic matter, the 'only relevant propositions that he formulates are propositions describing the nature of the work. And these are plain records of fact'. We might reasonably think, therefore, that the expressivist cannot capture disagreement since, on one standard view, two people 'cannot be truly said to disagree unless they are formally contradicting one another: unless one is asserting a 'genuine proposition' and the other is denying it, either directly or by implication' (Kivy 1980: 357).

So, how well can the expressivist account for disagreement? Some early expressivists, such as Ayer (1936: 111), are happy to bite the bullet here allowing that there is no genuine disagreement over matters such as aesthetics and ethics (though there could be genuine disagreements over factual matters concerning, for example, the nature and history of particular artworks). Ayer, for example, argued that there is 'no possibility of arguing about questions of value in aesthetics, but only about questions of fact' (1936). Other early expressivists demure, though, with Stevenson (1962) famously arguing that, in addition to straightforward factual disagreement, there is a further kind of genuine disagreement which he terms 'disagreement in attitude'. According to Stevenson (1962: 2), the 'difference between the two senses of "disagreement" is essentially this: the first involves an opposition of beliefs, both of which cannot be true, and the second involves an opposition of attitudes, both of which cannot be satisfied'. For example, if I have a strong pro attitude toward painting walls neon green and my flatmate (bizarrely) has a strongly anti attitude towards this, then our projects will quickly come into conflict. Similarly, two individuals with wildly clashing moral attitudes are likely to reach important practical impasses at various points. The plausibility of Stevenson's proposal has, of course, been subject to some debate (Hall 1947, Eriksson 2016) and, in particular, Kivy (1980: 357–9) has argued that it is significantly less plausible in aesthetics than ethics.

Regardless of the plausibility of Stevenson's approach, though, many contemporary expressivists would rebut this objection to their view at a much earlier stage, rejecting the claim that the expressivist cannot allow for propositional disagreement. To explain this further, Sinclair (2007: 347) uses the phrase 'propositional clothing' to denote a certain set of features which we might wish a kind of sentence to meet, features which include

> standards of appropriate and inappropriate usage; the ability to appear intelligibly in the linguistic contexts of negation, conditionalisation, disjunction and propositional attitude ascription; the warranted applicability of a truth-predicate; the ability to function in contexts of knowledge attribution; the ability to function as explaining phrases.

And, he notes, various key works in expressivism – going back at least as far as Stevenson (1962) and more recently including Blackburn (1988, 1998) and Gibbard (1992) – have gone to great lengths to argue that expressivists can 'vindicate these features for moral discourse' (1992: 348) and have at least suggested (Blackburn 2010) that similar moves can be applied in aesthetics. And, of course, the possibility for sustained and sensible disagreement looks (at least on the face of things) to be very much a feature of this kind. As with my discussion of contextualism earlier, though, I don't mean to take any particular stance on how successful the expressivist is at accommodating disagreement (faultless or otherwise). Rather, my aim has been to suggest two key claims in relation to expressivism. First, that the expressivist has multiple (at least prima facie plausible) strategies for capturing the possibility of disagreement. Second, that, as with subjectivism, the most attractive versions of contemporary expressivism allow for the possibility of substantive knowledge.

My aim so far has been to show that views such as expressivism and subjectivism can do a better job of capturing substantive notions of knowledge, as well as the possibility for disagreement, than we might initially think. Before moving on, though, it's worth briefly returning to the question of what the absolutist can say concerning the possibility of faultless disagreement. As discussed earlier, the absolutist can certainly allow for epistemically faultless disagreement but can they go further that this? Let's consider one approach. We saw in the last section that Hume's view in aesthetics depends heavily on the notion of true judges. However, Hume goes on to acknowledge that the judgements of these judges will sometimes diverge (1757 / 1875: 255). This has typically been taken as indicating something like faultless disagreement and is thought to raise the same kinds of problem for the absolutist we looked at earlier. Given that Hume takes the judgement of true judges to align with – and perhaps even constitute – correct aesthetic standards, we seem to be committed, if we adopt an absolutist semantics, to multiple incompatible standards. The case of true judges has received a great deal of subsequent attention (Budd 1995: 19–20, Kieran 2004: 228–9), but it has also been suggested that we need not interpret the divergence here as concerning genuine disagreement,

Shelley (2013: 146) suggests that 'Hume's considered view ... is that true judges will never disagree' and that the standard view to the contrary is mistaken.

> Because the standard reading does not regard Hume as marking a distinction between merely feeling and judging by feeling, it cannot regard him as marking a distinction between merely differing and disagreeing, and so must take him to be countenancing blameless disagreements in countenancing blameless differences. But the notion of a blameless disagreement is a muddle we ought not foist on Hume if we can help it. To say that two parties disagree is to say that at least one party is wrong. To say that their disagreement is blameless, in Hume's sense of the term, is to say that neither party is. If a twenty-year-old judges Ovid to be better than Tacitus while his fifty-year-old counterpart judges Tacitus to be better than Ovid, when Ovid is no better than Tacitus and Tacitus no better than Ovid, then both are wrong and their disagreement, evidently, is not blameless. (Shelley 2013: 146)

Whether the notion of blameless disagreement is really a muddle is, as we've seen earlier, a matter of some debate. However, Shelley's key claim is that 'Hume's considered view is the one according to which variation in predilections felt does not amount to disagreement in judgments made' (2013: 146).

Shelley relies here on there being two ways of interpreting divergence between ideal critics. On the first of these, there is a genuine disagreement between the two judges such that, say, one makes the aesthetic judgement that Ovid's work is greater than that of Tacitus and the other holds the reverse view. This would be a genuine disagreement, but Shelley denies this is something which, on Hume's understanding, can occur. On the other hand, there is a situation where both judge that these works are of comparable quality – or that they are in some way incommensurate – and their divergence is merely matter of personal preference.

Consider, for example, someone who finds themselves 'in the mood' for a light-hearted comedy movie one evening. It would seem strange to construe this as a judgement that such films are in any sense *better* than others or that their previous positive judgements about *Grave of the Fireflies* had been mistaken. On Shelley's interpretation of Hume's mature view, the judge who prefers the light-hearted comedy in no way takes their earlier self to be mistaken in their judgement, and the same would apply to, for example, someone's temperament giving them a lifelong preference for comedies over tragedies. By its very nature, of course, this move doesn't strictly allow the absolutist to accommodate faultless disagreement – we saw earlier that Shelley takes this idea to be a muddle – but it allows them to accommodate something very close which could easily be taken to cover many of the same intuitions (for further attempts to allow the absolutist to account for the appearance of faultless disagreement that aren't merely epistemic see Baker and Robson 2017, and Hills 2022: 34).

3.4 Non-absolutist Views, Aesthetic Knowledge, and Deference

We've seen that considerations of (apparent) disagreement don't provide any reason for taking aesthetic matters to be mere 'matters of opinion' in a way which undermines appeal to substantive investigations into aesthetic knowledge. Before we move on, though, it's worth explaining why I don't take any of the non-absolutist views discussed in this section – or at least any which contemporary aestheticians take to be live options – to undermine my previously mentioned faith in the epistemic power of (certain kinds of) aesthetic testimony.

I will use expressivism here as an illustrative example. It has been argued that expressivism is better able to accommodate pessimism than rival views (see, e.g., Blackburn 1998: 110 and Todd 2004) and some aesthetic expressivists are explicit in taking a rejection of deference as a starting point. Roger Scruton (1976: 54), for example, claims that his expressivist 'affective' theory of aesthetic judgement 'takes as its starting-point the intuition that, in matters of aesthetic judgments, you have to see for yourself' and recognise that 'another cannot make your aesthetic judgements for you'. However, we shouldn't be so quick to assume a link between expressivism and pessimism.

We saw earlier that expressivists have argued for fairly minimal standards for the existence of truth, knowledge, and so forth in a domain such as aesthetics. We have also seen that there are good reasons for those who adopt non-absolutist views of the aesthetic to still accept the thought that people can be mistaken in their own judgements, capable of improvement, and so on. Once we've gone this far, though, the idea that we should also defer to testimony becomes increasingly tricky to resist. For example, Fricker (2006: 225) suggests that we 'are essentially social creatures, and it is not clear that we do or could possess any knowledge at all which is not in some way, perhaps obliquely, dependent on testimony'. Similarly, Welbourne (1981: 302–303), maintains 'that knowledge is essentially commonable', in the sense that it is in the very nature of knowledge 'that it is capable of being transmitted from one person to another through speech or writing so as to become the common possession of two or more people' (Welbourne 1981: 302–303). Indeed, even if we rejected aesthetic knowledge (strictly speaking), as I think we should not, it's unclear whether this would go very far towards undermining optimistic views of aesthetic testimony. As Hills (2022: 23) points out, even

> if you are sceptical about aesthetic truth or aesthetic knowledge, it is overwhelmingly plausible that there are better and worse ways of forming aesthetic judgements. Good critics spend time becoming acquainted with the work of art, trying to understand it, and make their judgements of value based on that understanding. But if there are better or worse ways of making aesthetic judgements, then some critics may be better than you at making those judgements. For simplicity, we may call these better judgements true, and we will assume that the truths can be known (without a commitment to substantive aesthetic realism).

To say all of this is in no way to undermine views such as expressivism and subjectivism, since these can easily be made compatible with optimism. This is best seen by returning to the expressivism of Gibbard discussed earlier. Gibbard's (1992) main focus is on the moral case, and, as with the aesthetic case, he takes judgements here to express the acceptance of norms (in this case, roughly, norms permitting, forbidding or requiring particular actions). Gibbard (ibid. 174–88) is clear, though that there is no requirement that I choose which norms to adopt solely on the basis of my own first-hand judgement. Indeed, he is very careful about allowing room for deference to testimony, claiming that if 'under good conditions for judgment ... others find a norm independently credible. Then that must favor the norm in my own eyes' (Gibbard 1992: 180–181). And, although he is talking about moral norms here, I see no reason why he wouldn't also take this view to apply in the aesthetic case (especially since, as discussed in, e.g., Hills 2013 appeals to testimony in ethics are no less controversial than in aesthetics).

Of course, Gibbard's acceptance of the role of testimony is controversial, and I don't mean to suggest that no version of expressivism is compatible with rejecting the kind of deference being discussed here. Indeed, I've attempted elsewhere (Robson and Sinclair 2023) to develop a version of expressivism that is (for discussions of attempts to develop versions of other semantics which reject deference to testimony see Andow 2014). The point is, rather, that there are two challenges to be met here. First, the expressivist needs to thread the difficult needle of adopting various pieces of rival views' 'propositional clothing' (Sinclair 2007) as their own while, at the same time, keeping their view distinct enough from their rivals to claim that it allows a unique resistance to deference (I'm assuming here that the expressivist is looking to appeal to explanation that isn't equally available to rival views). Secondly, and more fundamentally, there's the question of whether the expressivist should even wish to do so. I hope to show in this work that there's good reason to take it that they should not.

3.5 Responding to Disagreement in Aesthetics

I've looked earlier at various theories about the nature of aesthetic judgement, and by extension aesthetic disagreement, noting that they have surprisingly little impact on questions of aesthetic knowledge. Before moving on, though, it's worth turning to a separate question about knowledge and aesthetic disagreement. How should we respond when we find out that those who are our peers, or even our superiors, when it comes to judging aesthetic matters disagree with us? I hope to have shown earlier that questions such as these can still arise (with, perhaps, a few relevant tweaks) even for those who endorse views such as subjectivism and expressivism. As such, questions of this kind will provide one relevant example of ways in which there can still be substantive questions of aesthetic knowledge on such views.

Before focusing on the aesthetic case, let's think about our responses to disagreement in general. One of the most prominent debates in early twenty-first-century epistemology has concerned how we ought to respond to disagreement with 'epistemic peers', that is, disagreement with those we take to be roughly our equals in terms of factors such as their general epistemic capabilities, track record, and the attention they have given to the issue in question (see Gelfert 2011 for a detailed discussion of epistemic peerhood). Consider the following famous case from David Christensen (2007: 193) involving disagreement between epistemic peers;

> Suppose that five of us go out to dinner. It's time to pay the check, so the question we're interested in is how much we each owe. We can all see the bill total clearly, we all agree to give a 20 percent tip, and we further agree to split the whole cost evenly, not worrying over who asked for imported water, or skipped desert, or drank more of the wine. I do the math in my head and become highly confident that our shares are $43 each. Meanwhile, my friend does the math in her head and becomes highly confident that our shares are $45 each.

How should we respond to disagreements of this kind? Importantly, the question being asked here isn't about how we should respond to any reasons that others give for their contrary judgement but merely how we should respond to the fact of disagreement itself. At one end of the spectrum there are those – such as Christensen 2007 and Elga 2007 – who argue for a strongly conciliatory view according to which disagreement of this kind should significantly shift our credence (typically suggesting that the rational thing to do in such a case is for both parties to move to a position of agnosticism about the issue in question). On the other extreme, the steadfast view (see, e.g., Kelly 2005, Weintraub 2013, Moon 2018) suggests that our credence in our judgements should vary very little, if at all, merely on the basis of peer disagreement. And, of course, there are also various intermediate positions. Further, while debates about how to respond to peer disagreement have been by far the most prevalent, there have also been controversies surrounding how to respond to disagreements with epistemic superiors (Frances 2010).

As we've seen with other debates in epistemology, though, it's commonly been suggested that aesthetics is different here. First, there is the question of whether our ordinary conceptions of peerhood in disagreement can be transposed to the aesthetic case. Pharr and Torregrossa (forthcoming: 31), for example, suggest that this may not be as straightforward as it seems and conclude their discussion by proposing that there is still 'much more that needs to be discussed about both the nature of aesthetic peerhood and the significance of aesthetic peer disagreement'. Secondly, and more prominently, it has been suggested that there are important differences in how we ought to respond to peer disagreement in aesthetics. Hopkins (2001: 169), for example, suggests that

> When one party finds herself disagreeing with several others who share a view, then (a) for ordinary empirical matters this is sometimes reason enough for her to adopt their view, but is never so in the case of beauty. Instead, in the

latter case (b) she should place less confidence in her view; and (c) she should, if possible, test the issue by re-examining the disputed item.

And others – such as McGonigal (2006) and Gorodeisky and Marcus (2018) – also endorse an asymmetry of this kind. We have seen that the correct response to disagreements about ordinary empirical matters is rather more controversial than these authors suggest, but are they right in taking the aesthetic case to be distinctive?

In order to answer this question, it's useful to consider two distinct stages. First, that of ceasing to hold your original belief. Second, that of coming to hold the belief of your opponent. The latter seems straightforwardly incompatible with various principles (such as the acquaintance principle) which we surveyed in the previous section. The first step is, however, entirely compatible with these principles. To come from believing an aesthetic claim to withholding judgement on the issue doesn't require forming any new aesthetic judgement, meaning that the acquaintance principle and its fellows are silent on our doing so. What should we make of this first step though? This question hasn't received anywhere near the attention as that of positively forming aesthetic judgements on the basis of testimony, but a common thought (Hopkins 2001: 168, McGonigal 2006: 332) is, again, that our response here should be less concessive than in other cases.

There are two concerns about taking an approach of this kind though. First, as discussed earlier, the issue of how to respond to peer disagreement in ordinary cases is more controversial than some of these writers suggest. And those who adopt relatively steadfast positions in the more general controversy could reasonably take any specific attempt to explain our unwillingness to defer in aesthetics to be otiose. Second, if we do take the aesthetic to be exceptional here, then it certainly seems as if we *could* produce views of aesthetic judgement which account for our unusual resistance to revising our original beliefs (and, e.g., Nguyen 2020: 1148 suggests a view of this kind). As with the testimonial case, though, the question arises as to whether we *should* wish to offer such accounts. That is, whether we should take there to be a relevant fact here to explain (see Robson 2014b for an argument that we shouldn't). I will return briefly to questions of the social epistemology of aesthetic judgement in §4.4, but, for now, let's move on to consider the final objection to my focus on aesthetic knowledge.

4 Aesthetic Knowledge: How to Get It and Why You Want It

This section will consider a final objection to the project of serious investigation into aesthetic knowledge. According to this objection, the concern is not that claims about knowledge of aesthetic properties are false or too easy to establish but, rather, that they are uninteresting. Mere aesthetic knowledge, the objector claims, isn't something we should (or typically *do*) have any significant interest in acquiring. To begin, I offer a more complete explanation of some of my views on the importance of aesthetic testimony which I have mentioned in previous sections. I then go on to argue that aesthetic knowledge, even (and sometimes especially) aesthetic knowledge acquired through social means such as testimony can be surprisingly valuable and plays an underappreciated role in our aesthetic practices. Finally, I go on to argue that the importance of social factors in acquiring aesthetic knowledge, and in our aesthetic practice more generally, extends far beyond cases of testimony.

4.1 Aesthetic Knowledge via Testimony

In previous sections I've made several references to the debate between the optimist and the pessimist. One surprising feature of these current debates is how rare it has become to see anyone defend the classic claim that we *cannot* acquire aesthetic knowledge via testimony. We saw in §2.1 that various claims such as the acquaintance principle have frequently been made – or at least interpreted – in epistemic terms. However, epistemic defences of pessimism are curiously hard to find (one exception is Whiting 2015, see Lord 2016 for a response). Rather, contemporary pessimists tend to endorse one of two broad strategies.

The first approach argues that aesthetic knowledge is possible on the basis of testimony but adds that there is some reason not to arrive at aesthetic knowledge in this way. The strongest version of this view, most prominently defend by Hopkins (2006, 2011, manuscript), maintains that some non-epistemic norm makes it impermissible to form aesthetic judgements on the basis of testimony. Other approaches tend to make significantly weaker claims. Hills (2022: 27), for example, merely maintains that

> An ideal aesthetic agent will have and use aesthetic understanding to make her aesthetic judgements, rather than base them on testimony, because an ideal aesthetic judgement will be based on the kind of grasp of aesthetic reasons characteristic of aesthetic understanding.

Similarly, Lord (2018: 71) argues that forming aesthetic judgements on the basis of testimony is 'non-ideal' but that 'there is no general obligation not to defer' to the testimony of others. I will return to these more modest strategies in §4.3 and suggest that they tend to underestimate the importance of aesthetic knowledge and underplay the role that such knowledge, including knowledge acquired via testimony, can play in achieving their proposed ideals. For now, though, let's think about the stronger version of the view. The standard concern for views of this kind is how to motivate the claim that there are, or even could be, additional norms of this kind on aesthetic judgement. As Hopkins (2011: 145) phrases the objection to his own proposal:

> Belief aims at truth, and aspires to the status of knowledge. Epistemic norms determine whether it hits this target. How can belief be governed by nonepistemic norms, norms that govern something other than whether it counts as knowledge? If someone's testimony offers one knowledge, how can one fail to mold belief to fit?

I have argued at length elsewhere that this objection is a significant one (Robson 2015) and that it may not even be coherent to take aesthetic judgements to be beliefs while also claiming that they're governed by norms beyond those which govern standard beliefs (Robson 2017). This, of course, raises the question of what happens if we don't take aesthetic judgements to be standard beliefs. This question leads us on to the second species of contemporary pessimism.

The other common approach for pessimists to take is to claim that, while aesthetic knowledge is attainable and is all that's required for beliefs formed in that way to be licit, aesthetic judgement is importantly distinct from aesthetic belief. Recall that, as discussed in §1.1, we're using 'aesthetic judgement' (as has become common in the literature) as a technical term to refer to whatever mental state(s) correspond to certain paradigm instances of aesthetic assertion. One way to deny that such judgements are beliefs would be to deny that we have aesthetic beliefs at all, but this isn't typically the approach which our second species of pessimist takes. Rather, they will often suggest that aesthetic beliefs exist but aren't the mental correlates of (the appropriate class of) aesthetic assertions (see Gorodeisky and Marcus 2018: 134–135). As discussed in §3.4, I am happy to allow that certain versions of this approach can exclude aesthetic judgements being legitimately formed, perhaps even formed simpliciter, on the basis of testimony. What we should ask, though, is whether we *want* to adopt a version of this kind. One of my key aims in this work is to highlight some reasons for thinking that we should not.

4.2 Optimistic in the Extreme

The position of the optimist in the debate surrounding aesthetic testimony has tended to be a rather defensive one, aiming to show that the deficiencies of testimony have been overstated. Even amongst optimists, though, it is readily assumed that testimony is lacking in some respects (Meskin 2006: 109) and even the most extremely optimistic views tend to be those which suggest that testimony is on an epistemic par with first-hand means of acquiring aesthetic knowledge (Laetz 2008, Robson 2022). I want to suggest, however, that there are actually reasons to take testimony (and similar social factors) to be our *best* means of acquiring aesthetic knowledge (for an extreme form of optimism about moral testimony, see McShane 2018).

Of course, I don't mean that any instances of testimony would always be epistemically superior to any instance of first-hand aesthetic judgement (such a view is implausible on its face). Rather, my suggestion is that the best that testimony can offer us is far better than the best which first-hand experience can offer. This might initially seem like a strange position to take. Surely, the very highest degree of warrant someone can transmit via testimony is the level of warrant which they themselves came to possess by some other means (such as first-hand perception). Lackey (1999: 471) describes this standard picture where testimony

> is like a chain of people passing buckets of water to put out a fire. Each person must have a bucket of water in order to pass it to the next person, and moreover there must be at least one person who is ultimately acquiring the water from another source. Similarly, each person in the chain of transmitting knowledge that p must know that p in order to pass it to the next person, and moreover there must be at least one person in the chain who ultimately acquired knowledge that p from another source, e.g., sense perception, introspection, reason, and the like.

Lackey's own view – and, I believe, the correct one – is that this standard picture is mistaken (see 1999: 471 and Graham 2006). However, I don't need to argue for any particular stance on these debates to make my case here.

To begin to see why, let's return to the issue of expertise in aesthetics. I have suggested (in §3.4) that, even if we adopt views such as subjectivism, there is a significant role for aesthetic experts. As such, it seems very plausible to think that we – that is, the majority of us who aren't bona fide experts in any aesthetic domain – could learn a great deal from, say, the testimony of one of Hume's 'true judges' that we couldn't learn merely from engaging with the work ourselves. (And this is without even mentioning the role such experts could play in helping us with more basic tasks of art appreciations such as identifying which works belong to a particular class and which works in that class are worth paying critical attention to.) This includes, but certainly isn't limited to, information about the work's aesthetic properties. These experts will, inter alia, have advantages over us in terms of their art historical knowledge, familiarity with similar works, perceptual capacities, and temperament for engaging with works of the relevant kind. Further, we should remind ourselves that we aren't restricted to receiving testimony from a single expert and, once we open up testimony from multiple sources, a range of further benefits arise. One key part of my defence here has already been offered in Section 2. Here I argued that the various concerns which arise regarding first-hand perception in aesthetics can be significantly ameliorated by relying instead on appeals to the test of time. And, while I suggested that the test of time isn't exclusively a matter of testimony (a point I will return to in §4.3), testimony, and especially expert testimony, certainly play a key role.

Further, these aren't the only epistemic benefits that we can reap from relying on aesthetic testimony. There are, as even the most casual observer will have noticed, a plethora of wildly varying artistic traditions (something which becomes even clearer when we think in global and historical terms). Further, it seems reasonable to suppose that making proper judgements for ourselves regarding these would require at least some level of experience and expertise. Even if we exclude those who are unable – owing to lack of ability, inappropriate temperament or whatever – to acquire the relevant expertise, though, it seems clear that getting to this stage is going to require a significant investment in terms of time and resources. Given this, there looks to be a limit to the number of artforms in which someone can acquire even a low-level expertise over the course of a lifetime (an anonymous referee for the press reminded me that this ties in with one possible understanding of the aphorism *ars longa, vita brevis*). Yet, there is no similar barrier to our accessing testimony from a range of different experts across artforms.

Still, we might think that the advantages I've highlighted here aren't especially impressive. I couldn't access *all* of these different pieces of knowledge myself, but I could access *any* of them. That is, there is no particular piece of knowledge which I could learn via testimony which I couldn't learn just as well on the basis of first-hand judgement. Similarly, I may not presently be an expert in evaluating any artform but there's no barrier to my becoming such if I so choose. We should remind ourselves, though, that the 'just as well' claim is mistaken and that, at least for certain kinds of testimonial knowledge I simply can't do just as well for myself. We have already seen this in the case of testimony from multiple individuals, as part of my discussion of the test of time, but the same also applies to testimony from a single person. One barrier to acquiring expertise is the commitment required but this this isn't the only one. It seems plausible to think that most of us could, with enough, acquire *some* level of expertise in any given artform but this doesn't mean that we could get anywhere close to the level of expertise which the best experts in those fields possess. Attaining this level of expertise may, for example, require exceptional perceptual capability, creativity in interpretation or the development of specific aesthetic virtues (for more on aesthetic expertise see Kieran 2011 and Lopes 2015). Further, with regard to some artforms at least, it seems plausible that the highest level of expertise may also require some expertise in producing the artform in question (Montero 2006). And, while putting the work in will certainly help in all of these areas, there is no guarantee that any given person will be able to succeed in any of them. Indeed, as with any skilled activity, there are likely to be those who – even correcting for equal amount of time, effort, and so on – stand out as exceptionally talented (Tolan 2019). And, by definition, most of us won't fall into this exceptional group.

Even if someone agrees with all of this, though, they might object that aesthetic knowledge is still a strange thing to focus significant attention on. I have talked a great deal here about how to acquire aesthetic knowledge but one natural concern to raise is why I should take aesthetic knowledge itself to be significant enough to be a worthy topic of extended study. After all, our interest in artworks isn't an interest in acquiring knowledge of the aesthetic qualities of the works, but, rather, it is an interest in experiencing and appreciating them.

It is important to be clear on the kind of epistemic benefit being dismissed as irrelevant here. There is a common idea in aesthetics that cognitive values play an important role in our engagement with art. For example, some have claimed that certain artworks can teach us important truths about human psychology and ethics, can help us learn cognitive virtues, and otherwise help us develop our epistemic agency (Kieran 1996, Carroll 2002, Young 2003, Erwenta et al. 2018). Further, this idea is typically taken further to propose that these cognitive benefits play a significant role in explaining the value of our engagement with artworks. For example, Young (1997: 21) suggests that 'The capacity of a work to contribute to human understanding gives us a standard against which we can evaluate aesthetic judgments'. These claims are, of course, controversial. As Christopher New (2002: 110) summarises some of these concerns, in relation to works of literary fiction, a work

> may well imply that the views are true, and do so very forcefully, but it cannot itself authenticate the view it conveys-whether the view is a sound one depends on what the (moral and religious) facts are, not on how the author's fiction represents them. So, while fiction literature may imply such truths, it cannot guarantee them. This does not mean, of course, that we cannot gather truths from fiction, only that they are not shown to be truths by virtue of being persuasively conveyed in a novel, story, poem, film or play. In this sense, claims that fiction has some kind of special route to moral (or any other) truth must be rejected as fanciful.

However, we need not settle things here for current purposes. The claim my opponent is making isn't the general one that cognitive states concerning artworks are irrelevant (and thus an unworthy area for study) but, rather, the much narrower claim that knowledge of the aesthetic properties of particular artworks is.

4.3 The Value of Aesthetic Knowledge

A first response to the aforementioned charge is that this isn't really an objection to anything that has been said thus far. It would be perverse to fault a guide to the waterfowl of Western Europe for your lack of interest in ornithology, and, similarly, everything that I've said so far about aesthetic epistemology could be perfectly true (fingers crossed) even if none of it is remotely interesting or important. Still, that's not exactly the result I'm hoping for.

In defence of the comparative (I mean, I'm not putting myself in contention for a Nobel Peace Prize here) importance of this project, it's worth noting that my hope is that most of the claims in this work will be of interest even to those who continue to believe that there is no particular value in the acquisition of aesthetic knowledge. By way of comparison, Gettier's famous (1963) paper remains of great interest to the majority of us who don't particularly value knowing what cars our colleagues own or how many coins strangers have in their pockets. I've suggested that various common claims about aesthetic epistemology are mistaken, and I believe that this should be of interest to anyone with an interest in either aesthetics or epistemology. Further, the claims I have been looking to reject aren't just obscure pieces of philosophical arcana but, as I have discussed, tend to also be common pieces of folk wisdom. Again, though, I don't want to overstate my case here, and I suspect that there is very little work in philosophy of art which, even in the unlikely event they chose to read it, would make a significant difference to the ways in which your average artist, art critic, or art consumer goes about their business (especially since, as discussed in §3.2, philosophers of art often seek to make their theories respect, rather than reform, current practice).

However, the main issue here isn't the self-referential discussion of the value of this work but, rather, the value of aesthetic knowledge itself. Here again, I think the case for the prosecution has been rather overstated and I will shortly go on to highlight some key ways in which aesthetic knowledge can be surprisingly important. To be clear, though, I certainly agree that the average audience for artworks isn't typically particularly interested in acquiring aesthetic knowledge when they open a new novel, visit a gallery, or purchase a ticket to the cinema. That's not to say that it *never* happens. Perhaps I really do just want to *know* whether *Madame Web* is quite as bad as I've heard or *learn* how successful a new friend is as a painter. Still, these are hardly typical cases. What exactly we are looking for in our typical engagement with art is a controversial topic and not one I will consider here (for some options see Young 2003, Dissanayake 2015 and Kieran 2004), but I agree that it is rarely mere knowledge of aesthetic truths. Given this, why think that aesthetic knowledge is valuable?

An easy response would be just to claim that aesthetic knowledge just has value in itself. That is, that such knowledge is intrinsically valuable. It seems, to some at least, plausible that any knowledge has some, perhaps not very impressive, level of intrinsic value (for some discussions of the value of epistemic states see Zagzebski 2004, Pritchard 2007 and Grimm 2008). Further, if we take certain aesthetic matters – such as whether a particular work is a masterpiece – to themselves be important, then we might also think that knowledge of these matters is more valuable than that of some trivial issue such as the precise number of blades of grass in a field. I do find these speculative claims rather attractive myself but don't want to stake my case on any of them. Claims about intrinsic value are not an easy matter to adjudicate, and I don't know of any good way to convince a sceptic here. Given this, I'm going to largely focus on cases where aesthetic knowledge looks to contribute towards other projects of value.

To begin, it's important to remember that the kinds of case considered earlier, of an ordinary art lover engaging with an artwork, are hardly the only cases there are. Let's consider two examples from Thi Nguyen. First, the case he calls (2017: 22–3) 'Instruction'.

> I am trying to decide what sort of musical education to give my child ... my child loves rap and wants to take some rap classes. I have my doubts – no matter how many albums my child plays for me, I just can't hear anything musically worthwhile. But my friend Roger, a professor of music theory and a wonderfully sensitive listener to all kinds of music, tells me that rap is actually a very complicated and musically valuable form. This sets my mind to rest – after all, what I really I want is for my child to *learn something worthwhile*, and the fact that Roger respects rap is far more telling than my own distaste. So I pony up and pay for my child to go to rap academy. (Italics mine.)

Second, the case he calls (Nguyen 2017: 26) 'Public Display' according to which

> I run a small local museum, and I am offered a chance to obtain a Turner painting for a very good price. I am assured by artists and art historians that I trust that the painting is of the utmost beauty and sensitivity, a real landmark. I study it for a long time, and fail to register its beauty in any way. But still, I trust my artist friends, the art historians, and especially the fact of their consensus, and hang the painting in my museum, not because I'm hoping to see the beauty for myself – I've given up on that – but because I am confident that *it is in fact beautiful, and that it does in fact contribute to the aesthetic value of the art contained in my museum*. (Italics mine.)

In both these cases, what seems important here is *knowing* the right things. Even if – contra Nguyen's own stipulation in Public Display – the people in these cases one day came to appreciate the works for themselves, this wouldn't seem to have any impact on how they should act. Pleasurable appreciation of the works might be a nice side benefit, but it is hardly the crucial aspect. Rather, they are interested in whether to pursue some other purpose – guiding their child's aesthetic education or deciding which works to display in their gallery – which they take to be (at least partially) contingent on the value of the works themselves. And decisions of this kind, where it seems appropriate to care about the value of works rather than our own individual appreciation of them, look to be surprisingly common in the artworld, encompassing decisions about what works to display, protect, study, subject to in-depth critical discussion, and so forth.

As an extreme example, consider the interesting case (discussed by Frowe and Matravers 2024) of protecting works of aesthetic or cultural significance during conflicts. Precisely how to balance such activities with other pressing concerns – most obviously protecting human lives – is certainly a complicated issue. However, the approach where individuals merely base their decisions on their own aesthetic preferences would clearly be a deeply flawed one. It's also worth noting that, while the examples discussed so far focus on works of high aesthetic value, these aren't the only kinds of works we might want to reliably identify. Educators and critics might well find it instructive to highlight works which are mediocre or outright terrible, historians of art might wish to highlight average works of a period rather than outstanding masterpieces (see, e.g., Ridley 1996 and Coll manuscript) and even empirical work in aesthetics itself will sometimes need to select works which differ in value (see Meskin et al. 2013).

To see why it is so important to consider the status of practices like these, let's consider an interesting claim which Hills makes in regard to the comparative importance of moral and aesthetic matters. Hills (2022: 33) suggests that, while moral errors can have a devastating impact, in aesthetics

> going wrong is typically not such a serious matter. If you fail to respond as the virtuous do, you will perhaps create or appreciate art that is not particularly valuable, take pleasure in the wrong aspects of a work of art; or judge works of art wrongly, or on the wrong basis.... Therefore, in aesthetics, even if your own aesthetic judgement is unreliable and you do not yet have aesthetic understanding, you do not have strong reasons to trust testimony instead. ... In aesthetics, the presumption in favour of making up your own mind is very strong.

Even though Hills (2009) is also sceptical about the value of moral testimony she thinks that there are clearly cases where – given the flaws in our own judgements and the urgency of the issue at hand – we would do best to rely heavily on it. By contrast, in the aesthetic case, she claims that while you should sometimes 'listen to the critics, and perhaps provisionally trust their judgements' there 'is very little pressure to defer to an aesthetic expert' (2022: 33). This lack of pressure to defer is further intensified when we consider the possibility that the works the ideal critics recommend to us, even if they are genuinely the ones with the highest levels of aesthetic value, need not be the ones which we ourselves would most enjoy (for discussion of this challenge see Levinson 2002). However, we have seen that, once we turn our gaze away from typical cases, the stakes can become much higher.

Claims about the value of aesthetic knowledge can, surprisingly, be reinforced by looking at some of the most influential objections to relying on aesthetic testimony. As was discussed in §4.1, a common theme in these objections is that relying on testimony to form our aesthetic judgements will provide us with knowledge but will fail to provide us with some further good. Let's suppose that we agree that something(s) other than knowledge is what's really important in aesthetic engagement. None of the candidates here look to be incompatible with our also acquiring knowledge via testimony. To see why, let's take aesthetic understanding as an example (a popular choice stressed by, e.g., Hopkins 2011, Lord 2018 and Hills 2022). To be clear, I'm not suggesting that we can come to *understand* why a work is beautiful merely by learning that it is beautiful on the basis of testimony (I agree that we cannot). Rather, the claim is that learning that something is beautiful on the basis of testimony isn't incompatible with later coming to understand that it is beautiful by encountering it for ourselves. Indeed, it isn't merely that knowledge isn't incompatible with our coming to do so, but, rather, it is actively helpful in doing so. Knowing that an object is beautiful will, so to speak, give us a head start on understanding *why* it is beautiful. Understanding is, after all, factive. Further, we are not just restricted to learning *that* an object is beautiful via testimony but can also learn various facts about the kind of beauty it instantiates, how it instantiates it and so on. In many cases even learning all of this won't take us as far as understanding since (as, e.g., Hills 2018 and Page 2022 highlight) aesthetic understanding is a demanding state to acquire and can often depend on very specific and idiosyncratic features of a work. I might come to know that, say, a work is particularly valuable because of the contrasts in the colour pallet, the mastery of perspective, and the vivid faces of the figures depicted. Still, knowing all of this won't enable me to understand *how* these features contribute to the value of the work. Again, though, they seem to help (rather than hinder) my ability to do so. Knowing 'where to look' is an important step towards developing such understanding, and helping us to do so has often (Lord 2019, Gorodeisky 2022) been highlighted as a key part of the role of the critic. Indeed, this is something that even those who are in other respects critical of the role of testimony recognise with, for example, Ransom (2019: 426) conceding that 'Aesthetic testimony can be vital to developing aesthetic competence as it can serve as a source of knowledge for novices who would otherwise be unsure of how to approach certain artworks, or even which artworks to engage with'.

It might be objected that this focus on individual cases is misguided and that the real issue is the general need to develop our own capabilities as aesthetic judges. This is the kind of view which Hills (2022: 24) takes when she focuses on the importance of developing aesthetic virtue considered as

> the orientation of the whole person towards aesthetic value and aesthetic reasons. Just as in the case of moral virtue, there are specific virtues, like honesty and courage, that are instances of this general idea. These are distinguished by being directed towards particular kinds of aesthetic value, or because the agent has to overcome specific kinds of obstacle to doing so or particular temptations to do otherwise.

Further, in Hill's view, we can only fully develop aesthetic virtue of this kind by engaging with artworks for ourselves. Again, though, none of this is (as Hills 2022. 30 notes) incompatible with our relying on testimony but rather with our *only* relying on testimony. Imagine that I'm seeking to train myself to be able to understand what makes a particular kind of musical composition graceful. In such a case, it would surely help to be pointed towards a range of relevant works which meet, as well as others which fail to meet, this descriptor. Of course, ideal training here will also likely involve some attempts to 'fly solo' by trying to evaluate a range of work about which I have no prior knowledge (testimonial or otherwise). This would, however, only be a counterexample to a claim – that we're *always* best placed relying on testimony – so extreme that even I have no intention of defending it.

One response here would be to consider the work of those, such as Nguyen (2020), who chart a more direct path to valuing autonomy. Nguyen (2020: 1127) takes us to be committed to the thought 'that, in aesthetic appreciation, we must form our own judgments for ourselves'. Nguyen doesn't take there to be any constitutive feature of aesthetic judgement which prevents deferring to the judgement of others or that renders such deference illegitimate. However, he argues (2020: 1138) that deference of this kind undermines a key value within our aesthetic practice and that we engage in the practice of seeking correct judgements in aesthetics 'for the sake of our involvement in the activity of seeking correct judgments, rather than for the sake of actually having made correct judgments'. In most other areas our investigations are just a means to an end, with that end being arriving at a correct judgement, but, in aesthetic matters, the 'primary value of the activity of aesthetic appreciation comes from the *process* of generating judgments and not the *end-product* – the judgments themselves' (for sympathetic discussions of, and challenges to, Nguyen's views here see Friend 2023 and Riggle 2024).

One concern here is whether the values Nguyen takes to be found in aesthetic investigation couldn't also be found in a process of aesthetic deference. As Riggle (2024: 398) phrases the challenge (for Riggle's own response to this challenge see Riggle 2024: 398),

> Surely adopting new beliefs about aesthetic value and pursuing their objects could be fun, lead to lively conversation, improve our understanding of other aesthetic points of view, and frame our ways of interacting with aesthetic objects in rich and rewarding ways, among other things. By adopting the aesthetic beliefs of others, we could kick off the pursuit of their objects, engaging with any and all aesthetic agents. Even better: in doing so our engagement is guaranteed aesthetic community with the source of our new aesthetic beliefs.

Further, even if we think the real value is to be had in autonomous investigation, acquiring aesthetic knowledge via testimony can play a surprisingly important role. Consider a comparison with playing a game such as chess (a comparison Nguyen 2020 frequently draws on). Any of us could, of course, improve our playing vastly by simply following the recommendations of a chessbot such as Stockfish. Further adopting this strategy would almost certainly lead to a victory (assuming our opponent wasn't opting for the same approach) and, if we could do so surreptitiously enough, we might even win ourselves some handy accolades and prizes in the chessworld. However, there's clearly a sense in which an approach of this kind would undermine the key values of chess playing. Naturally, the chess player sets their sights on victory, but, as with Nguyen's account of the aesthetic, much of the value is in the journey rather than the destination. Still, anyone with more than a casual interest in chess, and improving their chess game, will use chessbots. Not, of course, to play their games for them but to, for example, analyse alternative strategies, to check where a game went wrong or to identify what would have been the optimal move in a particular situation. Similarly, someone wanting to improve their 'play' when it comes to the game of autonomous aesthetic investigation will often have cause to defer to others as part of this training.

A final objection here is to claim that it is, in some sense, impermissible (and not merely non-ideal) to form aesthetic judgements on the basis of testimony because such judgements lack certain further features. For example, we've seen that Hopkins (2011: 149) proposes a non-epistemic norm which renders aesthetic judgements illegitimate in the absence of understanding. Views of this kind would certainly rule out legitimately forming aesthetic knowledge on the basis of testimony. There are, however (as I've already noted in §4.1), some prominent objections to views of this kind. Importantly, though, it's not even clear that – regardless of the status of objections to them – such positions do anything to impugn the value of aesthetic knowledge acquired on the basis of testimony. The idea that we can sometimes acquire valuable things by illegitimate means is, after all, hardly controversial. Even restricting ourselves to the epistemic domain, we may well acquire all manner of knowledge by stealing someone's private diary, bugging their phone, and bribing their acquaintances to disclose their secrets. The illicit nature of these activities does little (outside of, e.g., restricting its use in certain legal contexts) to reduce the value of the knowledge gleaned.

The examples I've discussed in this section will, hopefully, help to convince you that the idea that aesthetic knowledge is a singularly unimportant thing is mistaken. I don't mean to suggest here that aesthetic knowledge will *always* be important. I suspect, for example, that there is unlikely to be any circumstance where there will be much to be gained from my acquiring a comprehensive ranking of the aesthetic status of each blade of grass on my university's campus. Still, some knowledge in any field (no pun intended) is likely to be fairly unimpressive. What we have seen, though, is that there are cases where certain kinds of aesthetic knowledge can prove highly valuable.

4.4 Beyond Testimony

In this Element, I have argued that three influential claims about aesthetic knowledge are mistaken. Before finishing, though, I want to briefly consider what consequences this rejection might have for future work in the epistemology of aesthetics. There is much which could be said here but I want to focus on some ways in which we might further expand our work beyond a focus on first-hand perception and appreciation. I've spoken a great deal in this work about aesthetic knowledge in relation to testimony – reflecting the central role it has played within contemporary debates in aesthetic epistemology – but it's worth stressing that those of us interested in the social aspects of aesthetic knowledge shouldn't stop there. Testimony is far from being the only source of aesthetic knowledge that has been neglected in favour of a focus on first-hand perception and appreciation.

First, it is worthwhile to return to the broader kinds of deference I discussed in §2.5. Our ability to defer to others in the aesthetic cases, as with other domains, isn't limited to deferring to testimony alone. Rather, we could also consider deference to another person's judgements as expressed in various actions (the works they choose to purchase, to fill their home with, and so on) as well as, for example, non-verbal expressions or approval or disapprobation. I certainly believe that it's worth giving some consideration to the impact – epistemic and otherwise – of these broader kinds of difference. How much new philosophical light this shift in focus will shed, however, will depend on some broader debates on the nature of testimony. On a traditional approach, the focus on the epistemology of testimony has typically been on the reliability, in terms of competence and honesty, of the testifiers. That's not to say that there was a consensus on how we could arrive at such warrant, though, far from it. In particular, there were prominent debates concerning whether we need to have access to some positive reason for taking someone's testimony to be reliable or whether we had a 'default entitlement' to take it to be so (see Fricker 1994 for a defence of the former view and Coady 1992 for a defence of the latter). Recently, though, there has been significantly more focus on the 'interpersonal aspects' of testimony. According to these views (Leonard 2016:2334),

> the speech act of telling is key here. The basic idea is that in order for an audience to acquire testimonial justification (as opposed to inferential or perceptual justification, say), the speaker must *tell* her audience that p and the audience must *believe her* when she does. This is because when a speaker tells her audience that p, she is doing more than just making an utterance. Rather, she is *assuring*, or *guaranteeing* her audience that p is true; that is, she is *inviting the audience to trust her* when she says that p and is thereby offering to take responsibility for the truth of what she says.

If the former view is correct, then there is unlikely to be much deep difference between deferring to my testimony and deferring to, for example, the preferences I tacitly endorse through my actions. On the interpersonal view, though, the two are likely to be seen as fundamentally different. If I testify that a work is beautiful, then I am guaranteeing or assuring my audience that the work is beautiful in a way that I wouldn't be by merely tacitly endorsing the work by hanging it on my living room wall or unknowingly smiling in appreciation as I view it.

Another source of knowledge worth returning to is inference. As discussed in §2.5, principles of taste have received a fair degree of philosophical attention but other kinds of inference much less so (for more on the general status of inference in aesthetics see Cavedon-Taylor 2017). Let's consider one neglected kind of inference, inference from the aesthetic properties of other works by the same artist. One reason that has been suggested (Ridley 1996: 413) for widespread scepticism about inferences of this kind is a tendency of philosophers to focus on 'a list of canonical works, of undoubted masterpieces'. Works of this kind are often taken, by definition, to be 'something extraordinary, atypical, unprecedented' (Ridley 1996: 413) and will, therefore, often defy expectations even on the basis of the artist's other works. (Though even here, the case can be overstated. There are obvious similarities between, for example, Hitchcock's various cinematic masterpieces.) However, if we expanded our consideration to include what Ridley calls 'medium-grade' art (not to mention actively bad art), then the prospects for inductive inferences begin to look rather more rosy. Such works will, after all, often fall into familiar tropes for their genre, repeated favourite motifs of the artist and, in various other respects, be more likely to conform to expectations (which is not, of course, to suggest that less valuable works can never surprise us).

Considering the status of these neglected sources of aesthetic knowledge is certainly warranted, but I don't think that this is the only area where aesthetic epistemology could usefully be broadened. Rather, it is important to think about the role that social factors play in aesthetics more generally. It is very common for philosophers to write about aesthetic engagement as if it were typically a solo practice. However, this contrasts with the noteworthy fact of just how often our aesthetic engagements are group affairs. We frequently attend galleries, concerts, and the like – and even sit silently in cinemas and theatres – in the company of others (indeed, it is sometimes seen as eccentric to take part in some of these activities solo). Nor is this simply a matter of having pleasant company on these occasions (though no doubt that helps). Rather, we very often engage at length in what we might term 'aesthetic negotiation' (even Nguyen (2020: 1141) in his discussion of the value of autonomous aesthetic engagement also stresses the value of 'lovely, careful conversations' with others about aesthetic matters). That is, we take these occasions as springboards for discussions about the reasons why we hold our views of a work, why we are less convinced by the opposing views of our companions and so forth (we talk about the phenomenon at length in Wallbank and Robson 2022). This kind of aesthetic negotiation clearly isn't the only reason why aesthetic activities are so frequently communal – think of two friends silently spending time admiring a beautiful landscape – but it remains an important one.

Finally, I want to highlight that there have been many fascinating recent developments in social epistemology which have tended to go unexplored or underappreciated within aesthetics. There isn't time in what remains to do justice to the vast range of issues in social epistemology – including the epistemology of peer disagreement (already discussed in §3.5), the possibility of group knowledge (Lackey 2014a), and discussions of the epistemic privileges and disadvantages which certain social positions can generate (Toole 2021), but I will focus on a single representative example, the question of how to make our institutions better suited to the creation and transmission of knowledge (for some overviews of other debates in social epistemology see Lackey 2014b, Goldman 1999 and O'Connor and Goldman 2024).

There has been a great deal of work in social epistemology on how to improve the epistemic standing of various institutions. For example, how do we best arrive at knowledge of relevant facts in a legal setting and how do we balance this with other valuable considerations, such as ensuring that evidence isn't obtained by morally dubious means (Hoskins and Robson 2021). And, of course, the artworld is also formed of various institutions which focus on displaying artworks, preserving them, evaluating them, explaining them, and much more besides. However, there hasn't been much discussion in aesthetics of how these institutions can be improved from an epistemic perspective. In my view, one important explanation for this lies in the descriptive counterpart of some of the normative claims I've argued against in this Element. It is very common for aestheticians to take it for granted not only that we typically *ought* to only form aesthetic judgements on the basis of perception but also that we typically *do* only form such judgements in this way. Again, this view finds its most famous expression in Kant (1790/2012: 94) who, when discussing the situation of an individual faced with 'a hundred voices' all lauding a work, opines that this 'will not force his innermost agreement' since 'he clearly sees that the agreement of others gives no valid proof of the judgment about beauty' (Kant 1790/2012: 94). Given a view of this kind, the epistemic reach of various artworld institutions will be circumscribed in some key respects. They will, for example, draw works they take to be valuable to our attention, guide us in perceiving various aspects of the work itself, and provide training in the history and traditions of various artforms (I should be explicit that, while I don't take these to be *all* the artworld can do epistemically, I don't mean to suggest these tasks are insignificant). What they don't do is actually provide us with knowledge of the aesthetic properties of artworks.

Of course, given my normative claims earlier, you might expect me to argue that these institutions should be radically changed to start performing this further epistemic role. However, this is not the approach that I propose since I believe that this descriptive picture is also mistaken and that artworld institutions already play a significant role, for good or ill, in shaping people's aesthetic judgements. I have argued for a view of this kind at length in earlier work (Robson 2014a) and won't repeat these arguments in detail here. The main focus, though, was on engaging with empirical work which suggests that a surprising array of social factors – ranging from the testimony of critics to college rivalries – can have a wide-reaching impact on the aesthetic judgements that we form. Regardless of what we make of this descriptive point, though, those who agree with me in rejecting the normative point should be inclined to think – in the absence of a convincing argument to the contrary – that there is good reason to consider how best to improve the epistemic performance of various artworld institutions (either to help them to start performing this task or to improve their performance of it). I won't suggest details of how they might go about this here – though some of the examples already discussed in §4.3 might provide a useful starting point – but merely want to highlight the general lesson that there is much work to be done if we are to give full credit to the ways in which social factors can play a key role in the acquisition of aesthetic knowledge (and in our aesthetic lives more generally). Hopefully, this work will have helped to convince you of the importance of such a project.

References

Alcaraz Leon, M. J. (2008). 'The rational justification of aesthetic judgments'. *The Journal of Aesthetics and Art Criticism*, 66, 291–300.

Andow, J. (2014). 'A semantic solution to the problem with aesthetic testimony'. *Acta Analytica*, 30, 211–218.

Antipov, E. A. and Pokryshevskaya, E. B. (2017). 'Order effects in the results of song contests: Evidence from the Eurovision and the New Wave'. *Judgment and Decision Making*, 12(4) 415–419.

Arguello, G. (2019). 'Feminist aesthetics'. *International Lexicon of Aesthetics*.

Ashton, R. H. (2012). 'Reliability and consensus of experienced wine judges: Expertise within and between?' *Journal of Wine Economics*, 7(1) 70–87.

Ayer, A. J. (1936). *Language, Truth, and Logic*. London: Gollancz.

Baker, C. and Robson, J. (2017). 'An absolutist theory of faultless disagreement in aesthetics'. *Pacific Philosophical Quarterly*, 98, 429–448.

Barzman, K. E. (1994). 'Beyond the canon: Feminists, postmodernism, and the history of art'. *The Journal of Aesthetics and Art Criticism*, 52(3), 327–339.

Baumgarten, A. (1758). *Aesthetica*. Kleyb.

Brogaard, B. (2012). 'Knowledge-How'. In *Knowing how: Essays on Knowledge, Mind, and Action*, eds. J. Bengson and M. A. Moffett. Oxford: Oxford University Press, 137–160.

Beardsley, M. C. (1962). 'On the generality of critical reasons'. *The Journal of Philosophy*, 59, 477–486.

  (1981). *Aesthetics: Problems in the Philosophy of Criticism*. Indianapolis, IN: Hackett.

Bergqvist, A. (2010). 'Why Sibley is not a generalist after all'. *The British Journal of Aesthetics*, 50, 1–14.

Blackburn, S. (1988). 'Attitudes and contents.' *Ethics* 98: 501–517.

  (1998). *Ruling Passions*. Oxford: Oxford University Press.

  (2010). 'Truth, beauty and goodness'. In *Oxford Studies in Metaethics*, Volume 5, ed. R. Shafer-Landau. Oxford: Oxford University Press, 295–314.

Borge, S. (2019). *The Philosophy of Football*. Oxon: Routledge.

Bornstein, R. F. (1989). 'Exposure and affect: Overview and meta-analysis of research, 1968–1987'. *Psychological Bulletin*, 106(2), 265.

Budd, M. (1995). *Values of Art*. London: Penguin.

(2003). 'The acquaintance principle'. *The British Journal of Aesthetics*, 43, 386–392.

Calvo-Merino, B., Jola, C., Glaser, D. E., and Haggard, P. (2008). 'Towards a sensorimotor aesthetics of performing art'. *Consciousness and Cognition*, 17, 911–922.

Carlson, K. A. and Bond, S. D. (2006). 'Improving preference assessment: Limiting the effect of context through pre-exposure to attribute levels'. *Management Science*, 52(3), 410–421.

Carr, D. (2021). 'Narrative, knowledge, and moral character in art and literature'. *Journal of Aesthetic Education*, 55(3), 1–14.

Carroll, N. (2002). 'The wheel of virtue: Art, literature, and moral knowledge'. *The Journal of Aesthetics and Art Criticism*, 60(1), 3–26.

(2009). *On Criticism*. New York: Routledge.

Cavedon-Taylor, D. (2017). 'Reasoned and unreasoned judgement: On inference, acquaintance and aesthetic normativity'. *The British Journal of Aesthetics*, 57(1), 1–17.

Christensen, D. (2007). 'Epistemology of disagreement: The good news'. *The Philosophical Review*, 116(2), 187–217.

Citron, M. J. (1990). 'Gender, professionalism and the musical canon'. *The Journal of Musicology*, 8(1), 102–117.

Coady, C. A. J. (1992). *Testimony: A Philosophical Study*. Oxford: Clarendon Press.

Coll, C. (Manuscript). 'Form, content, and the case for bad literature'.

Cova, F., Olivola, C. Y., Machery, E. et al. (2019). 'De Pulchritudine Non Est Disputandum? A cross-cultural investigation of the alleged intersubjective validity of aesthetic judgment'. *Mind & Language*, 34(3), 317–338.

Cutting, J. (2006). 'The mere exposure effect and aesthetic preference'. In *New directions in Aesthetics, Creativity and the Arts*, eds. P. Locher, C. Martindale and L. Dorfman. Amityville, NY: Baywood, 33–46.

Davies, D. (2014). '"This is your brain on art": What can philosophy of art learn from neuroscience?' In *Aesthetics and the Sciences of Mind*, eds. G. Currie, M. Kieran, A. Meskin and J. Robson. Oxford: Oxford University Press, 57–74.

Davies, S. (1980). 'The expression of emotion in music'. *Mind*, 89(353), 67–86.

Davies, S. (1990). 'Replies to arguments suggesting that critics' strong evaluations could not be soundly deduced'. *Grazer Philosophische Studien*, 38, 157–175.

De Bruin, W. B. (2006). 'Save the last dance for me: unwanted serial position effects in jury evaluations'. *Acta Psychologica*, 118, 245–260.

De Clercq, R. (2008). 'The structure of aesthetic properties'. *Philosophy Compass*, 3(5), 894–909.
Dickie, G. (1974). *Art and the Aesthetic: An Institutional Analysis*. Ithaca: Cornell University Press.
  (1987). 'Beardsley, Sibley, and critical principles'. *The Journal of Aesthetics and Art Criticism*, 46, 229–237.
Dissanayake, E. (2015). *What Is Art For?* Washington: University of Washington Press.
Dorsch, F. (2017). 'Aesthetic reasons and aesthetic obligations'. *Estetika: The European Journal of Aesthetics*, 54(1), 3–19.
Douven, I. (2009). 'Uniqueness revisited'. *American Philosophical Quarterly*, 46(4), 347–361.
Dowling, C. (2010). 'The aesthetics of daily life'. *The British Journal of Aesthetics*, 50, 225–242.
Eaton, A. W. (2008). 'Feminist philosophy of art'. *Philosophy Compass*, 3, 873–893.
Egan, A. (2010). 'Disputing about taste'. In *Disagreement*, eds. T. Warfield and R. Feldman. Oxford: Oxford University Press, 247–286.
Elga, A. (2007). 'Reflection and disagreement'. *Noûs*, 41(3), 478–502.
Eriksson, J. (2016). 'Expressivism, attitudinal complexity and two senses of disagreement in attitude'. *Erkenntnis*, 81, 775–794.
Erwenta, J., Agung, L., & Sunardi, S. (2018). The values of character education in the didong Art performance: A study of enculturation process in Gayonese Society. *International Journal of Multicultural and Multireligious Understanding*, 5(4), 196–203.
Fechner, G. T. (1876). *Vorschule der Aesthetik*. Leipzig, Germany: Breitkoff & Hartel.
Ferretti, G. (2017). 'Pictures, emotions, and the dorsal / ventral account of picture perception'. *Review of Philosophy and Psychology*, 8, 595–616.
Frances, B. (2010). 'The reflective epistemic renegade'. *Philosophy and Phenomenological Research*, 81(2), 419–463.
Fricker, E. (1994). 'Against gullibility'. In *Knowing from Words*, eds. B. K. Matilal and A. Chakrabarti. Dordrecht: Kluwer Academic Publishers, 125–161.
  (2006). 'Testimony and epistemic autonomy'. *The Epistemology of Testimony*, eds. J. Lackey and E. Sosa. Oxford: Oxford University Press. 225–250.
Friend, S. (2023). 'Aesthetic appreciation without inversion'. *Aristotelian Society Supplementary Volume*, 97(1), 202–220.

Frowe, H. and Matravers, D. (2024). *Stones and Lives: The Ethics of Protecting Heritage in War*. Oxford: Oxford University Press.

Gelfert, A. (2011). 'Who is an epistemic peer?' *Logos & Episteme*, 2(4), 507–514.

Gettier, E. (1963). 'Is justified true belief knowledge?' *Analysis*, 23(6), 121–123

Gibbard, A. (1992). *Wise Choices, Apt Feelings: A Theory of Normative Judgment*. Oxford: Harvard University Press.

Ginsburgh, V. and van Ours, J. (2003). 'Expert opinion and compensation: Evidence from a musical competition'. *American Economic Review*, 93, 289–296.

Goldin, C. and Rouse, C. (2000). 'Orchestrating impartiality: The impact of "Blind" auditions on female musicians'. *American Economic Review*, 90(4), 715–741.

Goldman, A. H. (1993). 'Realism about aesthetic properties'. *The Journal of Aesthetics and Art Criticism*, 51(1), 31–37.

  (1995). *Aesthetic Value*. Boulder, CO: Westview Press.

  (2006). 'The experiential account of aesthetic value'. *Journal of Aesthetics and Art Criticism*, 64, 333–342.

Goldman, A. I. (1999). *Knowledge in a Social World*. Oxford: Oxford University Press.

Golub, C. (2017). 'Expressivism and realist explanations'. *Philosophical Studies*, 174(6), 1385–1409.

Gorodeisky, K. (2010). 'A new look at Kant's view of aesthetic testimony'. *British Journal of Aesthetics*, 50, 53–70.

Gorodeisky, K. (2021). 'The authority of pleasure'. *Noûs*, 55(1), 199–220.

  (2022). 'Must reasons be either theoretical or practical? Aesthetic criticism and appreciative reasons'. *Australasian Journal of Philosophy*, 100(2), 313–329.

Gorodeisky, K. and Marcus, E. (2018). 'Aesthetic rationality'. *The Journal of Philosophy*, 115, 113–140.

  (2022). 'Aesthetic knowledge'. *Philosophical Studies*, 179, 2507–2535.

Graham, P. J. (2006). 'Can testimony generate knowledge?' *Philosophica*, 78, 105–127.

Green, M. (2017). 'Narrative fiction as a source of knowledge'. In *Narration as Argument*, ed. P. Olmos, London: Springer, 47–61.

Grimm, S. (2012). 'The value of understanding'. *Philosophy Compass*, 7, 103–117.

Grimm, S. R. (2008). 'Epistemic goals and epistemic values'. *Philosophy and Phenomenological Research*, 77(3), 725–744.

Haan, M. A., Dijkstra, S. G., and Dijkstra, P. T. (2005). 'Expert judgment versus public opinion–evidence from the Eurovision song contest. *Journal of Cultural Economics*, 29, 59–78.

Hall, E. W. (1947). 'Stevenson on disagreement in attitude'. *Ethics*, 58(1), 51–56.

Hanson, L. (2013). 'The reality of (non-aesthetic) artistic value'. *Philosophical Quarterly*, 63, 492–508.

  (2015). 'Conceptual art and the acquaintance principle'. *Journal of Aesthetics and Art Criticism* 73, 247–258.

Hills, A. (2009). 'Moral Testimony and Moral Epistemology'. *Ethics*, 120, 94–127.

  (2013). 'Moral Testimony.' *Philosophy Compass*, 8(6), 552–559.

  (2018). 'Aesthetic understanding'. In *Making Sense of the World: New Essays on the Philosophy of Understanding*, ed. S. R. Grimm. Oxford: Oxford University Press, 160–176.

  (2022). 'Aesthetic testimony, understanding and virtue'. *Noûs*, 56(1), 21–39.

Hogan, P. C. (1994). 'The possibility of aesthetics'. *British Journal of Aesthetics*, 34(4), 1994.

Hopkins, R. (2000). 'Beauty and testimony'. In *Philosophy, the Good, the True & the Beautiful*, ed. A. O' Hear. Cambridge: Cambridge University Press. 209–236.

  (2001). 'Kant, quasi-realism, and the autonomy of aesthetic judgement'. *European Journal of Philosophy*, 9, 166–189.

  (2006). 'How to form aesthetic belief: Interpreting the acquaintance principle'. *Postgraduate Journal of Aesthetics*, 3, 85–99.

  (2011). 'How to be a pessimist about aesthetic testimony'. *Journal of Philosophy*, 108, 138–157.

Hopkins, R. (Manuscript). 'Norms of Use'.

Hoskins, Z. and Robson, J. (ed.) (2021). *The Social Epistemology of Legal Trials*. New York: Routledge.

Hume, D. (1757/1875). 'Of the standard of taste'. In *Essays Moral, Literary and Political*, ed. G. Richards, 142–154.

Irvin, S. (2014). 'Is aesthetic experience possible?' In *Aesthetics and the Sciences of Mind*, eds. G. Currie, M. Kieran, A. Meskin and J. Robson. Oxford: Oxford University Press, 37–56.

Isenberg, A. (1949). 'Critical communication'. *The Philosophical Review*, 58, 330–344.

Johnson King, Z. A. (2023). 'On snobbery'. *British Journal of Aesthetics*, 63(2), 199–215.

Kant, I. (1790/2012). *Critique of Judgement*. Trans. J. H. Bernard. New York: Dover.

Kelly, T. (2005). 'The epistemic significance of disagreement'. *Oxford Studies in Epistemology*, 1, 167–196.

Kennick, W. E. (1958). 'Does Traditional Aesthetics Rest on a Mistake?' *Mind*, 67, 317–334.

Kieran, M. (1996). 'Art, imagination, and the cultivation of morals'. *The Journal of Aesthetics and Art Criticism*, 54(4), 337–351.

(2004). *Revealing Art*. Oxon: Routledge.

(2011). 'Knowledge: Aesthetic psychology and appreciative virtues'. In *The Aesthetic Mind: Philosophy and Psychology*, eds. E. Schellekens and P. Goldie. Oxford: Oxford University Press, 32–43.

King, A. (2023). 'Response-dependence and aesthetic theory'. In *Fittingness: Essays in the Philosophy of Normativity*, eds. C. Howard, R. A. Rowland. Oxford: Oxford University Press, 309–326.

Kivy, P. (1980). 'A failure of aesthetic emotivism'. *Philosophical Studies*, 38, 351–365.

Köhler, S. (2012). 'Expressivism, subjectivism and moral disagreement'. *Thought: A Journal of Philosophy*, 1(1), 71–78.

(2017). 'Expressivism, meaning, and all that'. *The Journal of Philosophy*, 114, 189–207.

Kölbel, M. (2004). 'Faultless disagreement'. *Proceedings of the Aristotelian Society*, 104, 53–73.

(2009). 'The evidence for relativism'. *Synthese*, 166(2), 375–395.

Kompa, N. (2015). 'Contextualism and disagreement'. *Erkenntnis*, 80, 137–152.

Korsmeyer, C. (1979). 'Pictures and the relativity of perception'. *The Personalist*, 60(3), 290–297.

(2002). *Making Sense of Taste: Food and Philosophy*. New York: Cornell University Press.

Korsmeyer, C. and Weiser, P. (2021). 'Feminist aesthetics'. In *Stanford Encyclopedia of Philosophy*, ed. E. Zalta.

Kubala, R. (2023). 'The aesthetics of crossword puzzles'. *British Journal of Aesthetics*, 63(3), 381–394.

Lackey, J. (1999). 'Testimonial knowledge and transmission'. *The Philosophical Quarterly*, 49(197), 471–490.

(2006a). 'Knowing from testimony'. *Philosophy Compass*, 1, 432–448.

(2006b). 'The nature of testimony'. *Pacific Philosophical Quarterly*, 87, 177–197.

(2014a). 'Socially extended knowledge'. *Philosophical Issues*, 24, 282–298.

(ed.). (2014b). *Essays in Collective Epistemology*. Oxford: Oxford University Press.

Laetz, B. (2008). 'A modest defense of aesthetic testimony'. *The Journal of Aesthetics and Art Criticism*, 66, 355–363.

Lauter, P. (2013). 'Race and gender in the shaping of the American literary canon: A case study from the twenties'. In *Feminist Criticism and Social Change*, eds. J. L. Newton & D. Rosenfelt. New York: Routledge, 19–44.

Leonard, N. (2016). 'Testimony, evidence and interpersonal reasons'. *Philosophical Studies*, 173, 2333–2352.

Levinson, J. (2002). 'Hume's standard of taste: The real problem'. *The Journal of Aesthetics and Art Criticism*, 60(3), 227–238.

(2005). 'Aesthetic properties'. *Proceedings of the Aristotelian Society*, 79, 191–227.

(2009). 'The aesthetic appreciation of music'. *The British Journal of Aesthetics*, 49, 415–425.

Livingston, P. (2003). 'On an apparent truism in aesthetics'. *British Journal of Aesthetics*, 43, 260–278.

Logue, H. (2013). 'Visual experience of natural kind properties: Is there any fact of the matter?' *Philosophical Studies*, 162(1), 1–12.

(2018). 'Can we visually experience aesthetic properties?' In *Evaluative Perception*, eds. Bergqvist, A and Cowan, R. Oxford: Oxford University Press, 42–57.

Lopes, D. (1996). *Understanding Pictures*. New York: Clarendon Press.

(2011). 'The myth of (non-aesthetic) artistic value'. *The Philosophical Quarterly*, 61(244), 518–536.

(2014a). 'Feckless reason'. In *Philosophical Aesthetics and the Sciences of Mind*, eds. G. Currie, M. Kieran, A. Meskin and J. Robson. Oxford: Oxford University Press, 21–36.

(2014b). *Beyond Art*. Oxford: Oxford University Press.

(2015). 'Aesthetic experts, guides to value'. *The Journal of Aesthetics and Art Criticism*, 73(3), 235–246.

Lord, E. (2016). 'On the rational power of aesthetic testimony'. *The British Journal of Aesthetics*, 56, 1–13.

(2018). 'How to learn about aesthetics and morality through acquaintance and testimony'. In *Oxford Studies in Metaethics*, ed. R. Shafer-Landau. Oxford: Oxford University Press, 71–97.

(2019). 'The nature of perceptual expertise and the rationality of criticism'. *Ergo*, 6, 810–838.

MacFarlane, J. (2005). 'The assessment sensitivity of knowledge attributions'. *Oxford Studies in Epistemology*, 1, 197–233.

Margolis, J. (1960). 'Aesthetic perception'. *The Journal of Aesthetics and Art Criticism*, 19(2), 209–213.
  (1966). 'Sibley on aesthetic perception'. *The Journal of Aesthetics and Art Criticism*, 25(2), 155–158.
Marques, T. (2016). 'Aesthetic predicates: A hybrid dispositional account'. *Inquiry*, 59(6), 723–751.
Martindale, C., Moore, K., and West, A. (1988). 'Relationship of preference judgments to typicality, novelty, and mere exposure'. *Empirical Studies of the Arts*, 6(1), 79–96.
Matravers, D. (2005). 'Aesthetic properties I'. *Proceedings of the Aristotelian Society, Supplementary Volumes*, 79, 191–210.
Matthen, M. (2017). 'The pleasure of art'. *Australasian Philosophical Review*, 1(1), 6–28.
McGonigal, A. (2006). 'The autonomy of aesthetic judgement'. *The British Journal of Aesthetics*, 46(4), 331–348.
McGrath, S. (2009). 'The puzzle of pure moral deference'. *Philosophical Perspectives*, 23, 321–344.
McKinnon, R. (2017). 'How to be an optimist about aesthetic testimony'. *Episteme* 14, 177–196.
McShane, P. J. (2018). 'The non-remedial value of dependence on moral testimony'. *Philosophical Studies*, 175(3), 629–647.
Merli, D. (2008). 'Expressivism and the limits of moral disagreement'. *The Journal of Ethics*, 12(1), 25–55.
Meskin, A. (2004). 'Aesthetic testimony: What can we learn from others about beauty and art?' *Philosophy and Phenomenological Research*, 69, 65–91.
Meskin, A. (2006). 'Solving the Puzzle of Aesthetic Testimony.' In *Knowing Art*, ed. M. Kieran and D. McIver Lopes. Dordrecht: Springer, 109–124.
Meskin, A., Phelan, M., Moore, M., and Kieran, M. (2013). 'Mere exposure to bad art'. *British Journal of Aesthetics*, 53(2), 139–164.
Miščević, N. (2018). 'Predicates of personal taste: Relativism, contextualism or pluralism?' *Croatian Journal of Philosophy*, 18(54), 385–402.
Montero, B. (2006). 'Proprioception as an aesthetic sense'. *The Journal of Aesthetics and Art Criticism*, 64, 231–242.
  (2012). 'Practice makes perfect: The effect of dance training on the aesthetic judge'. *Phenomenology and the Cognitive Sciences*, 11, 59–68.
Montoya, R. M., Horton, R. S., Vevea, J. L., Citkowicz, M., and Lauber, E. A. (2017). 'A re-examination of the mere exposure effect: The influence of repeated exposure on recognition, familiarity, and liking'. *Psychological Bulletin*, 143(5), 459.

Moon, A. (2018). 'Independence and new ways to remain steadfast in the face of disagreement'. *Episteme*, 15(1), 65–79.

Mothersill, M. (1961). 'Critical reasons.' *Philosophical Quarterly*, 2, 74–78.

(1994). *Beauty Restored*. Oxford: Oxford University Press.

Nanay, B. (2016). *Aesthetics as Philosophy of Perception*. Oxford: Oxford University Press.

New, C. (2002). *Philosophy of Literature: An Introduction*. London: Routledge.

Nguyen, C. T. (2017). 'The uses of aesthetic testimony'. *The British Journal of Aesthetics*, 57, 19–36.

(2020). 'Autonomy and aesthetic engagement'. *Mind*, 129, 1127–1156.

(forthcoming). 'The aesthetics of drugs'. In *The Palgrave Handbook of Philosophy and Psychoactive Drug Use*, ed. R. Lovering. New York: Palgrave Macmillan, 631–651.

O'Connor, C. and Goldman, A. (2024). 'Epistemic Contextualism.' Stanford Encyclopaedia of Philosophy.

Page, J. (2022). 'Aesthetic understanding'. *Estetika*, 59(1), 48–68.

Palmira, M. (2015). 'The semantic significance of faultless disagreement'. *Pacific Philosophical Quarterly*, 96, 349–371.

Patridge, S. (2023). 'Aesthetic snobbery'. *Philosophy Compass*, 18, 1–8.

Perina, M. (2009). 'Encountering the other: Aesthetics, race and relationality'. *Contemporary Aesthetics*, 2, 1.

Pettit, P. (1983). 'The possibility of aesthetic realism'. In *Pleasure, Preference and Value*, ed. E. Schaper. Cambridge: Cambridge University Press, 17–38.

Pharr, Q. and Torregrossa, C. (forthcoming). 'Aesthetic Peerhood and the Significance of Aesthetic Peer Disagreement'. *Southern Journal of Philosophy*.

Plassmann, H., O'Doherty, J., Shiv, B., and Rangel, A. (2008). 'Marketing actions can modulate neural representations of experienced pleasantness'. *Proceedings of the National Academy of Sciences*, 105, 1050–1054.

Pritchard, D. (2007). 'Recent work on epistemic value'. *American Philosophical Quarterly*, 44(2), 85–110.

Radford, C. (1989). 'Emotions and music: A reply to the cognitivists'. *The Journal of Aesthetics and Art Criticism*, 47(1), 69–76.

Ransom, M. (2019). 'Frauds, posers and sheep: a virtue theoretic solution to the acquaintance debate'. *Philosophy and Phenomenological Research*, 98(2), 417–434.

(2022). 'Aesthetic perception and the puzzle of training'. *Synthese*, 200(2), 127.

Ridge, M. (2009). 'Moral assertion for expressivists'. *Philosophical Issues*, 19, 182–204.

Ridley, A. (1996). 'The philosophy of medium-grade art'. *British Journal of Aesthetics*, *36*(4), 413–423.

Riggle, N. (2024). 'Autonomy and aesthetic valuing'. *Philosophy and Phenomenological Research*, 109(1), 391–409.

Roberts, P., Andow, J., and Schmidtke, K. (2014). 'Colour relationalism and the real deliverances of introspection'. *Erkenntnis*, 79, 1173–1189.

Robson, J. (2013). 'Appreciating the acquaintance principle: A reply to Konigsberg'. *British Journal of Aesthetics*, 53, 237–245.

(2014*a*). 'A social epistemology of aesthetics'. *Synthese*, 191, 2513–2528.

(2014*b*). 'Aesthetic autonomy and self-aggrandisement'. *Royal Institute of Philosophy Supplement*, 75, 3–28.

(2015). 'Aesthetic testimony and the norms of belief formation'. *European Journal of Philosophy*, 23, 750–763.

(2017). 'Against aesthetic exceptionalism'. In *Art and Belief*, eds. Ema Sullivan-Bissett, Helen Bradley, and Paul Noordhof. Oxford: Oxford University Press, 213–229.

(2018). 'Is Perception the canonical route to aesthetic judgement'. *Australasian Journal of Philosophy*, 96, 657–668.

(2019). 'Aesthetic testimony and the test of time'. *Philosophy and Phenomenological Research*, 96, 729–748.

(2022). *Aesthetic Testimony: An Optimistic Approach*. Oxford: Oxford University Press.

Robson, J., & Sinclair, N. (2023). 'Speculative aesthetic expressivism'. *British Journal of Aesthetics*, 63(2), 181–197.

Romanos, G. D. (1977). 'On the" Immediacy" of art'. *The Journal of Aesthetics and Art Criticism*, 36(1), 73–80.

Saito, Y. (2015). 'Aesthetics of the everyday'. In *Stanford Encyclopedia of Philosophy*, ed. E. Zalta.

Savile, A. (1977). 'On passing the test of time'. *The British Journal of Aesthetics*, 17, 195–209.

(1982). *The Test of Time*. Oxford: Oxford University Press.

(2011). 'Perspective in Taste Predicates and Epistemic Modals.' In *Epistemic Modality*, eds. A. Egan and B. Weatherson. Oxford: Oxford University Press, 179–226.

Schafer, K. (2011). 'Faultless disagreement and aesthetic realism'. *Philosophy and Phenomenological Research*, 82(2), 265–286.

Schellekens, E. (2007). *Aesthetics and Morality*. London: Continuum.

(2008). 'Three debates in meta-aesthetics'. In *New Waves in Aesthetics*, eds. K. Stock and K. Thomson Jones. London: Palgrave Macmillan, 170–187.

(2009). 'Taste and objectivity: The emergence of the concept of the aesthetic'. *Philosophy Compass*, 4(5), 734–743.

Scruton, R. (1976). *Art and Imagination*. Methuen: London.

Scruton, R. (1979). *The Aesthetics of Architecture*. Princeton: Princeton University Press.

Sedivy, S. (2018). 'Aesthetic properties, history and perception'. *The British Journal of Aesthetics*, 58(4), 345–362.

Sen, S. (1998). 'Knowledge, information mode, and the attraction effect'. *Journal of Consumer Research*, 25(1), 64–77.

Shah, N. and Velleman, V. (2005). 'Doxastic deliberation'. *Philosophical Review*, 114, 497–534.

Shelley, J. R. (1998). 'The problem of non-perceptual art'. *The British Journal of Aesthetics*, 43(4), 363–378.

(2013). 'Hume and the joint verdict of true judges'. *The Journal of Aesthetics and Art Criticism*, 71(2), 145–153.

(2023). 'Aesthetic acquaintance'. *Pacific Philosophical Quarterly*, 104(2), 392–407.

Shelley, J. (2003). The problem of non-perceptual art. *The British Journal of Aesthetics*, *43*(4), 363–378.

Shin, N. (2022). 'Korean aesthetic consciousness and colour preference in clothing style'. *ESPES*, 11(1), 87–97.

Sibley, F. (1959). 'Aesthetic concepts'. *The Philosophical Review*, 68, 421–450.

(1965). 'Aesthetic and nonaesthetic'. *The Philosophical Review*, 74, 135–159.

(1968). 'Objectivity and aesthetics'. *Proceedings of the Aristotelian Society*, 42, 31–72

Silvers, A. (1991). 'The story of art is the test of time'. *The Journal of Aesthetics and Art Criticism*, 49(3), 211–224.

Simpson, M. (2020). 'What is global expressivism?' *The Philosophical Quarterly*, 70(278), 140–161.

Sinclair, N. (2009). 'Recent work in expressivism'. *Analysis*, 69, 136–147.

(2007). 'Propositional clothing and belief'. *The Philosophical Quarterly*, 57, 342–362.

Sosa, E. (1991). *Knowledge in Perspective: Selected Essays in Epistemology*. Cambridge: Cambridge University Press.

Stanley, J., & Williamson, T. (2001). 'Knowing how'. *The Journal of Philosophy*, 98(8), 411–444.

Stevenson, C. L. (1962). *Facts and Values: Studies in Ethical Analysis*. New Haven: Yale University Press.

Strawn, M. W., & Thorsteinson, T. J. (2015). 'Influence of response mode on order effects in the interview'. *Human Performance*, 28(3), 183–198.

Taylor, P. C. (2016). *Black is Beautiful: A Philosophy of Black Aesthetics*. Chichester: John Wiley & Sons.

Todd, C. S. (2004). 'Quasi-realism, Acquaintance and the Normative Claims of Aesthetic Judgement'. *British Journal of Aesthetics*, 44, 277–296.

Tolan, S. S. (2019). 'Profoundly gifted: Outliers among the outliers'. *The SAGE Handbook of Gifted and Talented Education*, SAGE Publications Inc., 104–116.

Toole, B. (2021). 'Recent work in standpoint epistemology'. *Analysis*, 81(2), 338–350.

Tormey, A. (1973). 'Critical judgments'. *Theoria*, 39, 35–49.

Wallbank, R. and Robson, J. (2022). 'Over-appreciating Appreciation'. In *Perspectives on Taste*, eds. J. Wyatt, J. Zakkou, and D. Zeman. New York: Routledge, 40–57.

Walton, K. L. (1970). Categories of art. *The Philosophical Review*, 79(3), 334–367.

Watkins, M. and Shelley, J. (2012). 'Response-dependence about aesthetic value'. *Pacific Philosophical Quarterly*, 93(3), 338–352.

Weintraub, R. (2013). 'Can steadfast peer disagreement be rational?' *The Philosophical Quarterly*, 63(253), 740–759.

Welbourne, M. (1981). 'The community of knowledge'. *The Philosophical Quarterly*, 31, 302–314.

Whiting, D. (2015). 'The glass is half empty: A new argument for pessimism about aesthetic testimony'. *The British Journal of Aesthetics*, 55, 91–107.

Wollheim, R. (1980). *Art and Its Objects*, 2nd ed. Cambridge: Cambridge University Press.

Young, J. O. (1997). 'Relativism and the evaluation of art'. *Journal of Aesthetic Education*, 31(1), 9–22.

(2003). *Art and Knowledge*. Routledge.

(2009). 'Relativism, standards and aesthetic judgements'. *International Journal of Philosophical Studies*, 17(2), 221–231.

Zagzebski, L. (2004). 'Epistemic value monism'. In *Sosa and His Critics*, ed. J. Greco, Oxford: Blackwell, 190–198.

Zajonc, R. B. (1968). 'Attitudinal effects of mere exposure'. *Journal of Personality and Social Psychology*, 9(2), 1–27.

Acknowledgement

I'd like to thank the editor, as well as two anonymous reviewers from the press, for very helpful comments on this Element.

Cambridge Elements

Epistemology

Stephen Hetherington
University of New South Wales, Sydney

Stephen Hetherington is Professor Emeritus of Philosophy at the University of New South Wales, Sydney. He is the author of numerous books, including *Knowledge and the Gettier Problem* (Cambridge University Press, 2016), and *What Is Epistemology?* (Polity, 2019), and is the editor of several others, including *Knowledge in Contemporary Epistemology* (with Markos Valaris: Bloomsbury, 2019), and *What the Ancients Offer to Contemporary Epistemology* (with Nicholas D. Smith: Routledge, 2020). He was the Editor-in-Chief of the Australasian Journal of Philosophy from 2013 until 2022.

About the Series

This Elements series seeks to cover all aspects of a rapidly evolving field, including emerging and evolving topics such as: fallibilism; knowing how; self-knowledge; knowledge of morality; knowledge and injustice; formal epistemology; knowledge and religion; scientific knowledge; collective epistemology; applied epistemology; virtue epistemology; wisdom. The series demonstrates the liveliness and diversity of the field, while also pointing to new areas of investigation.

Cambridge Elements

Epistemology

Elements in the Series

The Skeptic and the Veridicalist: On the Difference Between Knowing What There Is and Knowing What Things Are
Yuval Avnur

Transcendental Epistemology
Tony Cheng

Knowledge and God
Matthew A. Benton

Knowing What It Is Like
Yuri Cath

Disagreement
Diego E. Machuca

On Believing and Being Convinced
Paul Silva Jr

Knowledge-First Epistemology: A Defence
Mona Simion

Emotional Self-Knowledge: How Affective Skills Reveal Our Values, Goals, Cares and Concerns
Matt Stichter and Ellen Fridland

Deception and Self-Deception
Vladimir Krstić

The Epistemology of Logic
Ben Martin

The Indispensability of Intuitions
Marc A. Moffett

Aesthetic Knowledge
Jon Robson

A full series listing is available at: www.cambridge.org/EEPI

For EU product safety concerns, contact us at Calle de José Abascal, 56–1°,
28003 Madrid, Spain or eugpsr@cambridge.org.

www.ingramcontent.com/pod-product-compliance
Lightning Source LLC
LaVergne TN
LVHW011856060526
838200LV00054B/4367